Fitness for CHILDREN

Curt Hinson
Lancashire Elementary School
Wilmington, Delaware

Human Kinetics

Library of Congress Cataloging-in-Publication Data

Hinson, Curt, 1959-
    Fitness for children / Curt Hinson.
        p.   cm.
    Includes bibliographical references.
    ISBN 0-87322-472-8
    1. Physical fitness for children.   2. Physical education for
children.   I. Title.
    GV443.H47   1995   94-15898
    361.7'042--dc20   CIP

ISBN: 0-87322-472-8

Figures 1.2 and 1.3 adapted by permission of Polar Electro.

Acquisitions Editor: Rick Frey; **Developmental Editor:** Anne Mischakoff Heiles; **Assistant Editors:** Ed Giles, Jacqueline Blakley, Julie Marx, Kirby Mittelmeier; **Copyeditor:** Molly Bentsen; **Proofreader:** Jim Burns; **Typesetting and Layout:** Ruby Zimmerman; **Text Designer:** Jody Boles; **Cover Designer:** Jack Davis; **Photographer (cover):** Will Zehr; **Illustrator:** Patrick Griffin; **Mac Art:** Studio 2D; **Printer:** United Graphics

Human Kinetics books are available at special discounts for bulk purchase. Special editions or book excerpts can also be created to specification. For details, contact the Special Sales Manager at Human Kinetics.

Printed in the United States of America   10 9 8 7 6 5 4 3 2

Human Kinetics
Web site: http://www.humankinetics.com/

United States: Human Kinetics, P.O. Box 5076, Champaign, IL 61825-5076
1-800-747-4457

Canada: Human Kinetics, Box 24040, Windsor, ON N8Y 4Y9
1-800-465-7301 (in Canada only)

Europe: Human Kinetics, P.O. Box IW14, Leeds LS16 6TR, United Kingdom
(44) 1132 781708

Australia: Human Kinetics, 57A Price Avenue, Lower Mitcham, South
Australia 5062 (08) 277 1555

New Zealand: Human Kinetics, P.O. Box 105-231, Auckland 1
(09) 523 3462

To my sons, Taylor and Keegan

Contents

Preface

If you teach children or are a parent, you can't avoid noticing the activity levels and lifestyles of today's youth. Television and video games have replaced sandlot games for many children. Electronic toys have replaced balls and jump ropes. When discussing children's health, people use words like *heart disease*, *stress*, and *obesity*. The evidence is there; fitness is not a priority in the lives of many children. As each day passes, more and more children become victims of unmotivated, unhealthy lifestyles. Teaching children the importance of fitness and involving them in regular, vigorous activity has become an objective of significant concern to parents, teachers, and society in general.

If you work with elementary school–aged children, you have the opportunity to help children understand and appreciate fitness. Your success, however, depends on your methods. More than ever before you must approach your teaching with new ideas and continued enthusiasm. The old idea of jogging laps around the gymnasium or performing a few calisthenics before playing a sport or game does not teach children about fitness. Fitness needs to be taught year-round, with time from each physical education period devoted solely to fitness knowledge and fitness development. In fact, fitness may very well be the only subject matter within physical education that is taught all year long.

Fitness for Children provides you with effective, challenging, and enjoyable activities to improve physical fitness among children in kindergarten through sixth grade. The activities I present address four fitness components: cardiorespiratory endurance, muscular strength, muscular endurance, and flexibility. They are designed specifically for you to develop fitness in children while teaching important components and principles. Many of the activities require little or no equipment, and all are noncompetitive and offer challenges for children at their own levels. The emphasis of each activity is participation and movement—there are no scores to be kept, and there are no losers.

The book is divided into five chapters. Chapter 1, "Children and Fitness," covers four major topics. First, I offer an overview of children's fitness, including three of my concerns. Then you'll find three practical goals for teaching fitness in today's elementary school. I explain five health-related fitness components and how they relate to children, and finally cover basic fitness principles, training methods, and useful heart rate information. Depending on your experience, you can use this information to renew or expand your own fitness knowledge.

Chapter 2, "Strategies for Teaching Children Fitness," covers teaching techniques to help you implement the activities. Suggestions are included on class organization, behavior, motivation, and how to involve all children in an activity. I have tried to list practical tips I have encountered through my own physical education teaching experience.

Chapter 3 has drawings and descriptions of the exercises used in the activities. An exercise is a component within an activity. For example, push-ups is an exercise done in "Fitness Bag," which is the activity.

The next three chapters detail the activities themselves, with chapter 4 addressing cardiorespiratory endurance, chapter 5 muscular strength and endurance, and chapter 6 flexibility. Each description outlines the grade level the activity is best suited for; what to do before you begin; equipment; organizing the children and the equipment; implementing the activity; variations; teaching tips; safety tips; and a suggested follow-up homework assignment.

In the appendix you will find directions for how to make materials you need for several activities.

A glossary of terms at the end of the book will refresh your fitness vocabulary and familiarize you with key concepts.

Have you been searching for ways to incorporate a comprehensive fitness program into your curriculum? You will find in-depth, practical information and activities in *Fitness for Children*. As an educator, you will be able to make a difference in the lifestyles of the children you teach and set them on the road to healthy lives.

Acknowledgments

During the time it has taken me to finish this project many people and organizations have helped me. To each and every one of them I am truly grateful, for it has been their support that has enabled me to make this book a reality.

My most sincere thanks goes to my wife, Michele. Were it not for her help this book would not exist.

Many other individuals deserve thanks for helping me along the way. Thanks to Dr. Frank Fry and Brian Barrett for all their help, and especially for listening to me talk about my teaching philosophy; Dr. Steven Fertig for use of his fax machine; Ron Sayo for his computer expertise; Gregg Montgomery for his advice on becoming a better teacher; Scott Wikgren at Human Kinetics for letting me share my ideas; Rick Frey and Anne Mischakoff Heiles at Human Kinetics for their professional leadership and advice; Amy James at Polar CIC for help with the heart monitors; Lance Erdos for helping me design and implement Motion Pictures and Pennant Fever; Larry McDonald, Don Puckett, and Ambrose Brazleton for their inspiration and advice; and the late Muska Mosston for sharing ideas and professional friendship.

Thanks also to the following organizations: Delaware Association for Health, Physical Education, Recreation and Dance (AHPERD); New Jersey AHPERD; the National Association for Sport and Physical Education; the Council on Physical Education for Children; Brandywine School District; the faculty and staff of Lancashire Elementary School; and the Lancashire Parent-Teacher Association.

And, finally, a very special thank you to the children of Lancashire Elementary School, both past and present. They have been my inspiration over the years to put this book together. Without them this book could not exist. They are the greatest (and possibly most fit) children on earth!

How to Use This Book

I suggest you get familiar with the information in the first two chapters before beginning the activities. This will better enable you to understand how to use the activities to enhance learning among your students.

When choosing among activities remember that many of them require knowledge and experience in performing specific exercises. These exercises are explained in chapter 3. Begin your program by involving the children in these exercises in small doses. Add more exercises as they progress. Quite often the first attempt at an activity will be a learning period of its exercises and components. Don't get frustrated if the activity doesn't go as planned. Take it step by step, and teach the children as you go.

How much time you have to devote to fitness will determine how you use the activities. Most are designed to be used for 8 to 12 minutes; if you have allotted more time than that for fitness, simply combine several activities. For example, you might use Magic Box as a flexibility warm-up, then move on to Motion Pictures for a cardiorespiratory workout. Some of the activities are suitable for short, introductory warm-ups. Others are best used as complete fitness lessons or workouts to give the children hands-on experience with vigorous exercise. The length of time you use an activity will depend on your objectives and on the children's fitness, knowledge, and experiences.

Once you have selected which activity or activities to implement, gather the necessary equipment and materials. Many activities require task cards or circuit cards; samples and basic instructions are included in the activity description. To find out more about making these cards, refer to the appendix. If you have access to a laminating machine, use it to add durability to the materials you make. (I use laminated task cards and posters more than 5 years old that are still in good shape.)

At the end of each activity I provide a suggested homework assignment. These assignments can be very helpful in improving children's knowledge and ability related to fitness. Whether you hand out the assignment on paper or give it verbally, it is an excellent way to promote healthy attitudes and lifestyles. The best tip I can give regarding homework is to be consistent. If the children know they are going to be receiving homework assignments regularly, they are more likely to complete them.

Whether to hold children accountable for turning in their homework is up to you. I have tried several methods. I started out requiring parent signatures on the assignments; an assignment without a signature was considered incomplete. I kept a homework tally and used it as part of each student's physical education grade. More recently I have done away with parent signatures; now I give assignments that require children to write, draw, circle, list, or make something in conjunction with doing physical activity. Because the children are required to show me their work, I have a better idea of who is actually doing the assignments.

If you are like me, you will continually be looking for ways to improve activities as you use them. If you have any suggestions or unique adaptations, please share them with me. I would appreciate your input, especially if it helps to make fitness more fun and rewarding for children.

Part One

Getting Ready

Children and Fitness

An Overview of Children's Fitness

Are elementary-aged children (grades K-6) fit? For physical educators and other health professionals that is a very important question. Your answer undoubtedly depends on who you talk to, what you read, or in what capacity you work with children. Before you try to answer, however, let me discuss several concerns I have about children and fitness. My goal is not to provide you with an answer to our question but to have you think about the direction of your efforts.

Concerns for Children's Fitness

It isn't difficult to find information related to the fitness levels of children. What is difficult is deciding what to believe. The confusion over whether children are fit or unfit, active or inactive stems from several problems.

First, the definition of fitness and of being "in shape" has changed dramatically over the years. Tests of athletic and motor ability were once major determinants of fitness testing. Today's testing to determine fitness levels focuses instead on health-related components, such as cardiorespiratory endurance, muscular strength, muscular endurance, flexibility, and body composition.

A second source of confusion is disagreement over *norm-referenced* standards versus *criterion-referenced* health standards for fitness. Norm-referenced standards are determined by a reference group, a sample from the population for which the standards are generalized. Children's test results are compared against this group, and assumptions are then made about their fitness levels. Criterion-referenced standards, on the other hand, are developed using scientific data relating to what is determined to be healthy or to cause improved health. Children's test results are then compared to this health standard, not to the results of other children. Because of the difference in the standards, a child could be considered more fit in a particular area by one standard than in the same area by the other.

Finally, researchers are uncertain whether fitness and physical activity in children are related. It has been assumed that active children are more fit than inactive children, but studies comparing the two have failed to provide a clear or adequate understanding of this relationship (Rowland, 1990). Because children are active does not mean they are fit, nor does being inactive mean necessarily that they are unfit. It appears that children are generally born as healthy and fit individuals. As they grow, their levels of fitness change. Whether a child remains fit depends largely on environment, attitude, knowledge, and lifestyle. We have made assumptions about fitness, but more and better research on this topic needs to be conducted to prove us right or wrong.

The Fitness Continuum

So are children fit? It appears clear that an accurate answer to our question is elusive. Determining whether or not children are fit should not be the focus. We should direct our energy instead to moving children toward being more fit and living more fitness-oriented lifestyles.

I think you will agree that everyone, infant to adult, possesses some level of fitness. This level is as individual as personality, intellectual

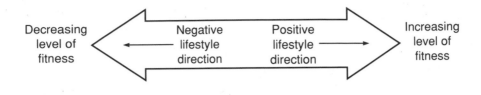

Figure 1.1   The fitness continuum: fitness as a process, not a product.

ability, and physical makeup. If fitness is thought of as a continuum with infinite ends (Figure 1.1), with everyone located at some point on it, where a person is located is his or her individual fitness level. This level can change, for better or for worse, and everyone's level moves continually in one direction or the other along the continuum.

Your goal as a fitness professional should be to teach children that their level is acceptable, wherever they are on the continuum, while at the same time encouraging them to move in a positive direction. In this approach, fitness is a process. If you develop standards that define fit and unfit in a limited way, children come to view fitness as a product instead of a process, and they tend to become discouraged if they seem to be far away from an acceptable level. Their perceptions have an enormous effect on whether they choose to move in a positive or a negative direction on the fitness continuum.

The Goals of Teaching Children Fitness

I have determined three primary fitness objectives that can be accomplished in limited teaching time. As you read on you will find that my goals are not product oriented. I don't aspire to have children run a mile in less than 10 minutes, or even to run a mile for that matter. I'm not concerned with whether they can do 1 pull-up or 20. My goals are process based and, for the most part, relatively simple. I want children to experience vigorous activity, learn to be self-responsible, and live healthy lifestyles.

If you could spend 30 to 45 minutes 5 days a week with the children you teach you would be able to accomplish many other fitness goals as well. Unfortunately, your time is probably limited to 1 or 2 days a week, and you need to teach many areas of physical education besides fitness. It's easy to focus on what can't be accomplished rather than what can. But take a moment to reconsider your objectives. If you focus on what you can accomplish in the time you have, you're more likely to be successful. Let me explain my three goals in more detail.

Goal #1: Vigorous Activity

It is well known that developing and improving cardiorespiratory endurance takes time. As you know, time is limited, so your chances of making enormous gains in a child's cardiorespiratory fitness level are remote. Instead of making this your goal, redirect your efforts to offer episodes of vigorous activity for the sake of the activity itself. The opportunity to engage in it is invaluable to children. It teaches them what their bodies are capable of and what it takes to improve the cardiorespiratory system. The experience of approaching anaerobic threshold, combined with brief explanations of what is taking place in the body, is an important part of the foundation children need to continue on their own.

Goal #2: Self-Responsibility

Everyone pursues fitness differently. I like to cycle, weight-train, and in-line skate. Perhaps you enjoy running, swimming, and playing tennis. Whatever it is, it's your own choice. Children need to learn that being fit is a choice they get to make. But to make it, they need to be self-responsible. You can't exercise for them, and you can't just give them fitness. Fitness must be earned by the person who wants it. Taking responsibility for one's own level of fitness is a critical step in developing lifelong fitness habits.

To ensure self-responsibility among children you must first make them feel comfortable with their current level of fitness. Next they need to realize that only they can change this level. And, finally, you must offer a variety of activities that capture their interest. If you can do this then children are more likely to continue their pursuit of fitness.

Goal #3: Healthy Lifestyle

Lifestyle is a matter of making decisions about how you want to live. It is based on selecting behaviors from choices you are confronted with. In a sense, it is a menu from which you choose what you want. The drawback of this menu is not so much that some choices cost more than others, but that the true costs of choices don't appear until years later. When an adult makes a lifestyle decision it is based on knowledge or experience that was attained since childhood. If the knowledge acquired has been beneficial and the experiences positive, perhaps the lifestyle decision will be a healthy one.

The lives of today's children present an abundance of choices related to physical fitness and health. To watch television or play a video game instead of going outside to kick a ball around is just one example of the decisions a child makes daily. Repeatedly choosing sedentary activities moves the child in a negative direction along the fitness continuum. Children need information on how to make healthy lifestyle choices. They need appropriate knowledge and experiences involving health-related fitness components and their benefits. You can provide these.

Health-Related Fitness Components

Components of physical fitness are divided between motor fitness and health-related fitness. Motor fitness has played a large role in fitness testing since President Eisenhower in the 1950s established the President's Council on Youth Fitness (now called the President's Council on Physical Fitness and Sports). In recent years, however, motor fitness has become less important in determining overall fitness levels. Since the 1980s the physical education profession has focused on what are called health-related fitness components, believed to better measure a person's overall fitness. They include cardiorespiratory endurance, muscular strength, muscular endurance, flexibility, and body composition.

Cardiorespiratory Endurance

Cardiorespiratory endurance (CRE), probably the most often cited component of physical fitness, involves the ability of the heart and lungs to supply oxygen to the working muscles for an extended period. The greater my CRE, the longer I can sustain aerobic activity.

CRE is determined by a concept called $\dot{V}O_2max$, or maximum oxygen uptake. How much oxygen a person can consume determines $\dot{V}O_2max$. In adults $\dot{V}O_2max$ is the primary method for measuring CRE, but its validity as a reliable measurement of children's CRE has not been determined (Rowland, 1990).

Muscular Strength

Muscular strength is the amount of force a muscle can exert in a single contraction. The benefits of increased muscular strength include reduced risk of injury and improved posture, physical performance, and body composition. Developing strength requires working against a resistance in a progressive manner.

Although most young children are physically incapable of developing large muscle mass at early ages, muscular strength can be improved. Implemented correctly, resistance training can be beneficial for children. The American Orthopaedic Society for Sports Medicine recommends several key elements to support a successful resistance training program for children before puberty: proper supervision; an emphasis on dynamic concentric contractions as opposed to eccentric overload exercises; use of a full range of motion; no competition; and the participant's emotional maturity toward the program (Cahill, 1988).

Muscular Endurance

Muscular endurance is the ability of a muscle to sustain a contraction or perform numerous contractions over an extended period. Improving muscular endurance requires continued use of a muscle or groups of muscles. The longer a muscle is used, the greater its endurance becomes. Muscular endurance is best enhanced when the muscle is required to perform 20 or more repetitions of an exercise or to sustain an activity for several minutes. Of course, for a muscle to function this long the work load must be minimal.

In young children, calisthenics and locomotor movements help to develop muscular endurance. When these types of activities are repeated on a continual basis, children become more efficient in their movements and can sustain activity longer. Being able to participate in activity for longer periods without muscle fatigue is the primary objective of developing muscular endurance in children.

Flexibility

Flexibility is the range of motion that can be achieved by a joint. This range is affected by several factors:

- Body temperature
- Elasticity of muscles, tendons, and ligaments

- Amount of fatty tissue around the joint
- Anatomical structure of the joint
- Injury

Flexibility, like fitness, is individual. Flexibility even differs within the same person; usually one side of the body is more flexible than the other. This can result from "handedness"—using one side of the body more than the other.

Flexibility can be improved by stretching. Muscle fibers respond to stretching and become longer, thus improving the range of motion that can be achieved. There are four basic types of stretching: static, dynamic, proprioceptive neuromuscular facilitation (PNF), and ballistic. The flexibility activities in chapter 6 use static and dynamic stretching. To give you a better idea of how they work, I will briefly explain each of the four here.

Static Stretching

Static stretching, the most popular type, helps children become more flexible. It involves stretching a muscle to a point of tension and holding it for 10 to 60 seconds. The longer a static stretch can be held, the more effective it is. With young children, however, it is best to start with short episodes. An important consideration during static stretching is not to stretch into the "discomfort zone," when the muscle begins to feel pain. When pain occurs the point of tension has been increased too far.

Young children have a difficult time with static stretching at first. Because they are unfamiliar with what a stretched muscle feels like, they quickly enter the discomfort zone. You can notice this right away because of the moaning and screaming (mostly exaggerated) that accompany the activity. To help avoid this, try to explain the feeling to the children before you begin. Because you cannot feel what they are feeling, it is best to let them decide when they have stretched far enough. Only time and experience with the feeling will enable students to comprehend the concept.

Dynamic Stretching

Dynamic stretching involves movement around a joint; it is an ideal way to involve children in flexibility. The range of motion can be enhanced by moving the joint in a continuous manner through its complete range of motion. The key to dynamic stretching is *slow* and *con-*

trolled movement. Excessive jerking or quickness can harm the muscle fibers.

Dynamic stretching is somewhat easier to get children to perform without excessive complaining about being in the discomfort zone. The difficult part is keeping them moving in a slow, controlled manner. With young children it is helpful to play "slow motion." Simply ask the children to do all their movements as slowly as possible without coming to a complete stop. Teaching children to stretch with a combination of static and dynamic stretches also helps bring about the concept of slow and controlled. An important point to make is that stretching should be done in a relaxed state.

Proprioceptive Neuromuscular Facilitation

In PNF stretching two people work together to stretch; one person stretches while the other (the helper) offers resistance. The helper moves the person stretching into a static stretch position and holds. The person stretching then applies force against the stretch in the form of a isometric muscular contraction. The helper resists the force and holds the person in the static stretch position. After a few seconds the isometric contraction is released and the helper attempts to increase the range of motion of the static stretch. This procedure has been found to be very effective in improving flexibility, but it takes knowledge and technique that are probably out of the realm of a young child's ability and perhaps beyond his or her needs.

Ballistic Stretching

Ballistic stretching involves actively moving the muscle while in a static stretch position; it can best be described as "bouncing." The problem with ballistic stretching is that the momentum from the bouncing or quick movements causes muscle fibers to go beyond their limits. The result is damaged or torn fibers. It is best to warn children about the dangers of ballistic stretching and explain it as the way *not* to stretch.

Body Composition

Body composition, usually expressed in a percentage of body fat, is the ratio of lean body mass to body fat. The most popular means of measuring percent body fat in the educational setting is with skinfold calipers. Calipers are used to measure the thickness of subcutaneous fatty tissue in several areas of the body, including the triceps, biceps, calf, iliac crest, and subscapular area. These measurements are then used to determine an estimate of overall body fatness.

It hardly seems necessary that young children be aware of the estimates of their body fat percentages, especially because several factors affect the reliability of the measurement. What is more important for children to understand is that their bodies store fat, which is needed for survival. Children need also to learn that the body will store fat in excessive amounts if they let it. They must learn that body composition is something they can influence through positive lifestyle choices of diet and exercise.

The Basics of Fitness

Russell Pate (1983) has recommended that promoting skills, knowledge, and long-lasting positive attitudes toward health and physical fitness should be a primary goal of children's fitness programs. To ensure children acquire all three, it is important to instill knowledge of concepts and principles related to fitness. Of course the level at which these concepts are presented depends on the capabilities of the children. The earlier children are exposed to the basics of fitness, the better the chance that this knowledge will become integral to their lives.

I have divided the basic concepts and principles necessary to better understand fitness into four categories: fitness principles, the workout, training methods, and listening to the heart.

Fitness Principles

Earlier in this chapter I mentioned that fitness should be viewed as a process of moving in a positive direction along the fitness continuum (as shown in Figure 1.1). In order for the process to make positive movement, several principles need to be adhered to.

Overload

Overload refers to the amount of exercise that is needed to improve fitness levels. For the body to improve it must be made to perform harder than it is accustomed to. This additional exercise can be considered a stepping stone to another level of achievement. If the body is never required to work at an overload level, then the best that can be achieved is to maintain a current level of fitness.

To explain overload to children it is best to let them experience it firsthand through vigorous activity. Have children keep track of how long they sustain an activity or how many repetitions they complete in a specified time. After several weeks of working on the same task, compare together their initial data with the new data. Ask them questions about their experience: Is it easier now to participate at your initial level? Why can you do more repetitions now in the same amount of time? What took place each time you participated in the activity? For children to discover the appropriate answers to these questions, you will need to guide them as they participate in the activity.

Progression

Progression is how overload should take place. An increase in the level of exercise, whether it be to run farther or to add more resistance, must be done in a progression. This enables the body to slowly adapt to the overload, thus eventually making the overload normal. Once this is achieved, progression is continued toward a new overload. If the progression is too fast or too intense, the body simply will not be able to work at the new level, and improvement may not occur.

Children need to understand that improving their level of fitness is an ongoing process. To help children better understand progression and see that they are improving, give them opportunities to track their progress. This can be accomplished with pretests and posttests of certain abilities. For example, before beginning work on flexibility have children complete a sit-and-reach test. After they do several weeks of flexibility activities, along with completing regular homework assignments related to flexibility, repeat the test. Afterwards, question the children on the results of the tests and why such results occurred.

Frequency

Frequency refers to how often a person engages in exercise activity. There are several standards for how frequently exercise should take place for improvement to occur. The most popular guideline, recommended by the American College of Sports Medicine (1990), is a minimum of three to five times a week. This guideline, however, was established for adults. It is unclear whether children need to follow this same standard to show improvement. More research needs to be conducted in this area.

Intensity

Intensity refers to how hard a person exercises within a given exercise period. Intensity depends on the fitness goals of the exerciser and the type of training method being used. In cardiorespiratory activities intensity is determined by speed. In muscular strength and endurance activities, intensity is related to the amount of resistance being used.

Teach children that intensity is directly related to how long they can sustain an activity. Understanding this concept takes time, especially when it involves pacing techniques. Children have a tendency to want to do everything fast and be the first one finished. The quality of their performance will suffer if their intensity is beyond their limits.

Duration

Duration is the amount of time a person participates in an exercise episode. In cardiorespiratory endurance activities such as running, duration is the amount of time spent running or the distance covered. In muscular strength and endurance activities, duration is based on the total number of sets and repetitions performed or the length of the total workout.

Have children time themselves with stopwatches while they participate in activities to help them grasp the idea of elapsed time. Very young children (grades K-2), though, generally have little concept of time, so don't feel you must get them to fully understand what duration means.

Workout

A workout is an episode in which someone tries to influence fitness by maintaining or improving cardiorespiratory endurance, muscular strength, muscular endurance, flexibility, body composition, or some combination of these. Whatever components are being focused on, every workout should include three phases: warm-up, conditioning, and cool-down.

Phase 1: Warm-Up

The warm-up phase raises the heart rate so that muscles and other tissues can be supplied with blood. Warm-up should focus on the same muscle groups that will be used in the conditioning. It is critical in helping to decrease risk of injury during the workout.

When you use the activities in this book, lead students in a warm-up activity beforehand. As you go through chapters 4, 5, and 6 you will find that several activities of short duration can be used as warm-ups for other, more vigorous activities.

Phase 2: Conditioning

The purpose of conditioning, the core of the workout, is to maintain or improve the current level of one or more fitness components. It is during conditioning that fitness gains are made; the duration depends on the goal. A typical cardiorespiratory endurance workout for adults would include 20 to 60 minutes of conditioning, but children can't usually sustain activity for that long. Keep in mind that the time constraints of the typical physical education class make improving fitness an unrealistic goal. Focus instead on helping children understand that the conditioning phase is where vigorous activity takes place.

Phase 3: Cool-Down

Cool-down is necessary to allow the body to slow down gradually. This facilitates the removal from the body of carbon dioxide and lactic acid, which are products of muscular contractions. The cool-down is critical in helping the body recuperate from conditioning activity. Failure to cool down sufficiently leads to muscle stiffness and soreness.

Make it a point to involve children in a slow, controlled activity at the end of your fitness lesson. Children tend to fall to the ground to rest when they have finished a vigorous activity, but you can discourage this by using a simple cool-down activity like stretching or walking.

Training Methods

Three different training methods can be used in performing an activity for fitness benefits. Each method has a distinct purpose; the goal of the workout determines the type to be used.

The first method is *continuous training*, in which the same activity or exercise is continued over an extended period, with endurance the usual objective. For example, you might involve the children in Frizz-B Fren-Z (see p.76) for 10 minutes, with the objective of having them do a vigorous cardiorespiratory endurance activity.

The second training method, *circuit training*, uses a number of different exercises at assigned stations. The stations are arranged so that children move from one to the next, usually in a circular sequence (hence the name circuit). This method lets you mix exercises of different intensities or specificities. You also can influence the intensity of the circuit by controlling the amount of time allotted to complete it.

The third method of training, *interval training*, alternates short bursts of high-intensity exercise with periods of rest. The purpose of this training is to push the body to a higher level of fitness. In cardiorespiratory endurance activities this consists of exercising to a point of *anaerobic threshold*, when the muscles' demand for oxygen is greater than what the cardiorespiratory system can supply. Interval training is useful when you involve children in cardiorespiratory endurance activities because it follows their natural tendency to exert themselves in short bursts of high intensity, then rest until they feel able to continue.

Listening to the Heart

Since the early 1980s, monitoring heart rate during exercise has become popular. It isn't uncommon to see an exerciser, with two fingers against the carotid artery in the neck, slowing down to look at a watch or clock. The positive correlation between heart rate and $\dot{V}O_2$max makes heart rate a good gauge of exercise intensity; by counting the heart rate, you can maintain an appropriate intensity for achieving cardiorespiratory benefits.

The Basics of Heart Rate and Exercise

Heart rate is stated as the number of times the heart beats in 1 minute (bpm). The rate at which your heart beats during exercise determines which energy system your body uses and what type of fitness you develop.

Resting heart rate is the rate at which the heart beats when a person is at complete rest. The best time to determine resting heart rate is before getting out of bed in the morning. The average resting heart rate for adults ranges from 60 to 80 bpm; children's is slightly higher. The rate for the average 8-year-old ranges between 80 and 100 bpm.

Maximum heart rate is the maximum number of beats the heart can beat in 1 minute. Maximum heart rate can be determined very accurately in a medically supervised stress test or by doing a high-intensity 1.5-mile run, but a simpler method is to subtract one's age from 220, referred to as the Karvonen method (1957). This estimate is sufficient for your purposes in teaching children, and I will explain it in more detail in a moment.

The heart rate reserve refers to the range between resting and maximum heart rate. For example, a 10-year-old with a resting heart rate of 80 has a heart rate reserve of 130 (220 – 10 = 210; 210 – 80 = 130).

The target heart rate refers to the heart rate needed to gain a training benefit. The target heart rate is divided into five different levels, or zones, based on the percentage of maximum heart rate achieved. Each zone represents a different type of training.

- Zone 1: 50% to 60% of maximum heart rate. This level is used for extended periods of exercise with the purpose of building endurance. The body will burn fat as fuel at this level.
- Zone 2: 60% to 70% of maximum heart rate. This level is also used to build endurance, while helping to strengthen the heart. It is a zone of moderate intensity that allows the exerciser to continue for an extended period.
- Zone 3: 70% to 80% of maximum heart rate. This level, known as the target heart rate zone, is where optimal aerobic training takes place. Overload occurs and aerobic gains are maximized in this zone.
- Zone 4: 80% to 90% of maximum heart rate. This level, referred to as the anaerobic threshold zone, is where the body reaches anaerobic threshold and begins working anaerobically, as opposed to aerobically. Interval training usually takes place in this zone.
- Zone 5: 90% to 100% of maximum heart rate. This zone is referred to as oxygen debt, meaning that the cardiorespiratory system can no longer supply the muscles with the oxygen they need to sustain movement at the current pace. Pushing yourself into this zone can be dangerous if you are not extremely fit. I use heart monitors to determine when children have reached this zone; however, children who get to this point usually stop on their own because of the fatigue they are experiencing.

Using the Karvonen Method

The most popular, as well as the simplest, way to determine target heart rate is the Karvonen method (1957), based on $\dot{V}O_2max$ scores and their correlation with heart rate. The following formula is used for the calculation:

> 220 – age = maximum heart rate
> maximum heart rate – resting heart rate = heart rate reserve
> (heart rate reserve × training zone percentage) + resting heart rate
>   = target heart rate

For example, figuring Zone 3 for a 7-year-old with a resting heart rate of 90 bpm would look like this:

$220 - 7 = 213$
$213 - 90 = 123$
$(123 \times 70\% \, [.70]) + 90 = 176$
$(123 \times 80\% \, [.80]) + 90 = 188$
Target heart rate Zone 3 = 176 to 188 bpm

This particular child would need to sustain a heart rate of 176 bpm to 188 bpm to exercise in Zone 3, which represents 70% to 80% of maximum heart rate. This formula can be used to calculate any of the five training zones by multiplying the percentages that correspond with the desired zone.

Using Heart Monitors with Children

Measuring heart rate to monitor exercise intensity in children is a relatively new and growing trend. Now with the emergence of accurate, wireless heart monitors, children can monitor their heart rates and learn the concept of exercise intensity. Involving children in experiments related to heart rate and exercise performance can teach them the value of a heart-healthy lifestyle (Hinson, 1994).

Wireless heart monitors offer children hands-on experience with what is happening to their hearts during physical activity. Children as young as first grade can learn fundamental principles of heart physiology and the heart's function during exercise (Hinson, 1994).

Heart monitors come in several different types in a price range of $90 to $390. The different functions the monitor can perform determine the cost. The most effective (and most expensive, at $390) model for the educational setting is the Polar Vantage XL. This model lets you download exercise data into a computer (software and computer interface are an additional $500). The computer software allows you to perform several different functions. For example, you can print heart rate graphs similar to the one shown in Figure 1.2. This line graph represents the heart rate of a 10-year-old during a 30-minute exercise episode. The two horizontal dotted lines represent Target Heart Rate Zones 2, 3, and 4 (60%-90% of maximum heart rate) for this particular child. In the data at the bottom of the graph, you see the child averaged a heart rate of 169 bpm during the episode while achieving a maximum heart rate of 201 bpm.

The computer software also lets you compare different exercise episodes and track cardiorespiratory performance. Figure 1.3 displays bar graphs that compare the time the child spent in Zones 2, 3, and 4 dur-

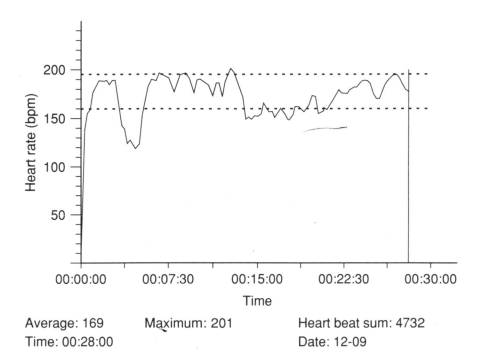

Heart Rate Curve

Average: 169   Maximum: 201   Heart beat sum: 4732
Time: 00:28:00   Date: 12-09

Figure 1.2   A 10-year-old's heart rate during a 30-minute exercise episode.

ing four different class periods. With this feedback children can visually comprehend the output of their hearts during exercise, and you get an indication of cardiorespiratory development.

Wireless heart monitors are a great tool for helping children understand the intensity levels necessary to maintain and improve cardiorespiratory fitness. Heart monitors also help you evaluate the activities you are using to engage the children in vigorous activity. Such information is invaluable in teaching children about the cardiorespiratory system.

When using heart monitors with children it is important to begin by teaching them basic heart physiology. Depending on their abilities, children can learn the path of the blood through the body, the blood's purpose, the difference in heart rate during rest and exercise, and more. This knowledge allows use of the monitors to be more beneficial. (The

American Heart Association offers a valuable teaching kit called "Getting to Know Your Heart" with posters, stethoscopes, and other materials. Contact your local chapter for information.)

With heart disease still the leading cause of death in the United States, this type of data certainly offers valuable fitness information. Children who are given the opportunity to work with such data are more capable of understanding how exercise affects their bodies. This alone supports the use of heart monitors within the fitness curriculum.

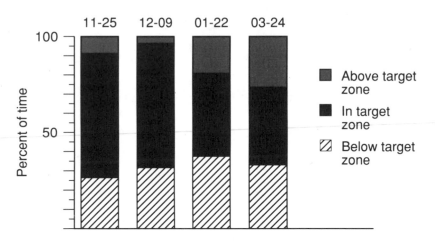

Figure 1.3 A comparison of four different exercise episodes using heart monitor data.

Strategies for Teaching Children Fitness

Teaching children fitness is not an easy job. It requires a well-planned and well-organized learning environment utilizing an array of teaching strategies. The strategies you use to implement a fitness program are based on your philosophy, your objectives, and the children you teach. To help you implement your program, I have included suggestions related to four areas: class organization, children's behavior, inclusion, and motivation. Think about these suggestions as you plan and execute your program.

Class Organization

Fitness is an ongoing process that deserves enormous attention. It can no longer be thought of as a unit that is taught for 6 weeks of the school year, then put away until the next year. Each class period should include some time devoted solely to fitness. Giving children regular, consistent experiences with fitness helps teach them the importance of daily exercise. It also promotes the concept of fitness as a process.

The amount of time you spend on fitness depends on your objectives for a particular lesson and the ability of the learners. Through my own experiences with involving children in fitness activities, I recommend you devote approximately 25% of class time to fitness. For typical elementary physical education classes, ranging from 30 to 45 minutes, this would be 8 to 12 minutes. At times you may plan several fitness activities or objectives, which will require additional time. This is certainly acceptable. In fact, it may be more conducive to learning to devote entire class periods to fitness, then use the shorter episodes to reinforce what was learned. This flexibility is helpful when a new concept, principle, or activity is being introduced.

If 8 to 12 minutes on fitness once or twice a week seems hardly long enough to teach children about fitness, don't get frustrated. Other aspects of your lessons will undoubtedly offer opportunities to reinforce fitness learning. Use activities, games, and skill practice during other class time to promote fitness. This procedure will work to your advantage and offer maximum results.

When to implement fitness activities into lessons is strictly a personal choice. Some educators prefer to begin class with a short warm-up activity, then move into a more vigorous fitness activity. Others prefer engaging children in skill development activities first, then fitness activities afterward. There is no correct sequence or formula. Your decision should be determined by your objectives, the learners, and the other activities you wish to include in the lesson.

Planning the class format is a vital link to the success of your program. You should spend time thinking of how best to organize the lesson based on your goals. After you have devised your plan, try it and evaluate it. Make any necessary changes that may be needed to improve the format. Often changing the sequence of the lesson's activities can improve the children's performance. If you seem to never be satisfied with how lessons turn out, don't give up—that's a sign that you are in search of excellence.

Children's Behavior and Self-Responsibility

When children misbehave or refuse to remain on-task, many teachers try to persuade them to conform to an acceptable standard (one the teacher has determined). A child who continually refuses to conform to the standard is then punished in some way, the purpose being to change the unacceptable behavior to that which is acceptable. This is known as behavior modification. It is an efficient and effective way of dealing with discipline problems, especially when managing a large group of children. But behavior modification, although effective in establishing conformity, may teach children very little in regard to self-responsibility.

Misbehavior from children is usually a signal that some aspect of your lesson is not to their liking. Although most children will not demonstrate this, there are usually a few who display it rather noticeably. Psychologist Abraham Maslow (1971) says that most of us have learned to avoid authenticity. In other words, we do not always show exactly how we feel. When children misbehave, often they are showing you how they truly feel. A child who is off-task is most likely demonstrating an attitude about the activity. Other children may be feeling the same way but be unwilling to display the same authenticity. The compliant child who believes that he or she must please the teacher is conforming to the teacher-established criteria. This behavior usually is a rewarded response, whereas misbehaving is not rewarded. As a result, some activities "work" because the children feel they must do them to please the teacher, but they probably are not being enjoyed by everyone.

Changing misbehavior often requires only a slight change in the way you present an activity. Trying to get children to conform is not the solution. Instead your focus should be on what it is that caused the noncompliance. By changing the environment, offering alternatives, and letting children give input, you can establish self-responsibility. When children have a sense of being able to think and act for themselves, many behavior problems are eliminated. The next two sections of this chapter offer ideas on how to accomplish this.

Teaching for Inclusion

Inclusion refers to having all children involved in an activity for its duration at a level that is appropriate to their individual needs and abilities. It is a concept made popular by Muska Mosston with his slanted rope experiment (Mosston & Ashworth, 1990). Mosston found that when children tried to jump over a rope held horizontal to the ground, some were eliminated because they could not clear the rope. A rope held on a slant, however, gave every child a suitable place to jump over. The principle behind inclusion is to challenge all children at the level that they decide is appropriate to their ability. When this challenge occurs, the potential for growth and development is greatly enhanced.

Inclusion is a very important component of any fitness lesson. When selecting a fitness activity for inclusion, you must answer two questions. Are the children able to select levels of participation that match their individual abilities? Does the activity involve all children all the time?

When a fitness activity offers a low personal challenge, children become bored. When the challenge is too high, they become frustrated. Both attitudes are detrimental to developing healthy lifestyles. In addition, children who spend time waiting in line for a turn to participate are offered less opportunity for growth. (Note: Some interval training activities in chapter 4 require that children take turns participating. Waiting a turn is actually the rest period needed to successfully complete a set of intervals.)

Fitness activities that are not inclusive should not be used with young children. Asking children to sit out or to participate at levels below or beyond their abilities causes them to become callous toward physical activity. If a particular activity cannot be adapted to offer inclusion, then you should not use it. But most activities, with the correct adaptations, can offer inclusion.

Extrinsic and Intrinsic Motivation

For years educators have used extrinsic motivation to persuade children to participate in activities and learning. Perhaps you have used it yourself. Rewards are the most common type of extrinsic motivator: certificates, stickers, grades, free time, patches, food, ribbons, and so on.

Intrinsic motivation, on the other hand, means doing an activity for personal enjoyment and for the sake of conquering a challenge. Participation is not centered on an award, recognition, or other external rewards.

Extrinsic Motivation

Extrinsic rewards can encourage participation, help children work to their full potential, and recognize success. Although rewards do promote achievement of these goals to some extent, there are drawbacks to consider.

When teachers use extrinsic rewards to control or manipulate children into participating in activities that they might have chosen to do on their own, then children view the rewards as the reason to participate (Raffini, 1993). In relation to fitness activities, then, if a child participates knowing a reward awaits at the completion of the activity, the child's focus is on participating for the reward and not for personal satisfaction or accomplishment.

When children participate in fitness activities,for recognition or rewards, they tend to view fitness as a product instead of an ongoing process. If we reward children for achieving particular fitness standards, for example, they may believe that once they have received their rewards, they can stop working at fitness. The process ends because the product has been received.

According to Raffini (1993), "extrinsic rewards in themselves neither undermine nor support intrinsic motivation; it is how they are used that matters" (p. 76). When extrinsic rewards are used as a motivator to persuade children to participate or to achieve a specific standard, then they do not promote intrinsic values. When children choose to participate on their own and experience feelings of competence, extrinsic rewards help reinforce those feelings. This in turn enhances their intrinsic motivation to participate in the activity. The key, however, is to introduce the extrinsic rewards in the correct manner. The best solution is to avoid using the rewards as the focus of the activity. If children do not know that rewards will be given, their effort and participation will not depend on them.

Intrinsic Motivation

Instead of relying on extrinsic rewards, work to make the activities you teach more intrinsically appealing. This takes careful selection and planning of the activities and the environment. When children participate in fitness activities for intrinsic reasons, they view fitness as a process. It becomes an ongoing activity that leads to personal satisfaction and competence.

According to Lepper and Hodell, and to Malone and Lepper, intrinsically motivating activities have four characteristics in common: challenge, curiosity, control, and creativity (cited in Raffini, 1993). Choosing and arranging activities so that children can experience each of these is important in helping foster intrinsic motivation. There are several considerations concerning the implementation of these characteristics in fitness activities.

First, you must teach on the basis of inclusion. All children must be involved at the level of challenge that meets their individual needs and abilities. Remember, if a challenge is too difficult, the child will become frustrated; if it's too easy, the child will become bored. Bored and frustrated learners often require extrinsic motivation to be convinced to participate; for them the activity offers no intrinsic motivation. Though you can coax participation with rewards, it is far better to change the level of challenge to better meet the need of each child.

Second, intrinsically motivating fitness activities need to provoke children's curiosity. Raffini (1993) says that "children possess a natural inquisitiveness about activities and situations that are novel or inconsistent with their experiences or expectations" (p. 70). When an activity arouses curiosity, a child becomes more motivated to partake for the sake of satisfying the curiosity. The curious child participates for her or his own reasons, not yours.

Third, children need to feel a sense of control over the activity and the environment. The more decisions children make within an activity, the more control they have. Giving children control and decision-making power teaches self-responsibility, which, as I mentioned in chapter 1, is one of the goals of the fitness program.

Finally, children need to be able to be creative and to fantasize about the content of the activity. This makes the activity fun, while giving children a chance to use their creative thinking skills. When children can create and fantasize they are better able to associate the activity with personal experiences. This relationship makes the activity more meaningful and relevant.

By now you are probably ready to move on and begin implementing the fitness activities in chapters 4, 5, and 6. That is OK, but you will benefit if you take a few moments to review the various exercises described and illustrated in chapter 3. Many of the activities, as you will see under the heading *Before You Begin*, require the children to have prior experience with these exercises. If you take the time now to familiarize yourself with the different exercises, you will have a better understanding of what is required to implement each activity.

Exercise Descriptions

Before you begin using the fitness activities in Part II, the children will need to learn some basic exercises and aerobic steps. All of these can be found in this chapter. They are ordered to correspond to chapters 4 to 6, with cardiorespiratory endurance exercises coming first and flexibility exercises, or stretches, coming last. For each exercise you will find a brief description and an illustration of a child performing it.

Cardiorespiratory Endurance Exercises

Some of the cardiorespiratory endurance activities in chapter 3 require the children to perform aerobic dance steps and step aerobics exercises. You will want to familiarize the children with these steps before incorporating them into your activities.

Aerobic Dance Steps

There are 12 aerobic dance steps. The children need not learn these in any set order, nor do they need to learn them all at one time. Depending on the level of the children, teach them a few steps at a time, then add more as they progress.

1. Bounce and Twist

Bounce up and down with feet together, twisting the upper body opposite to the lower body.

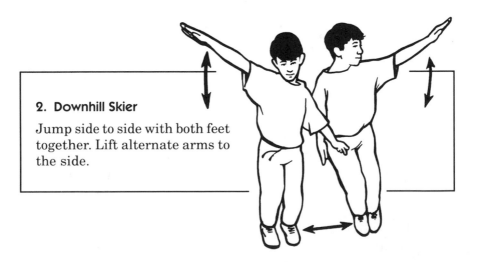

2. Downhill Skier

Jump side to side with both feet together. Lift alternate arms to the side.

3. Elbow to Knee

Alternate lifting the knees, touching each with the opposite elbow.

4. Hopscotch

With hands on the waist, hop in place, alternating feet. Bend the lifted knee to the back with each hop.

5. Jumping Jacks

Stand erect with arms at sides. Jump up, landing with feet apart and arms extended overhead. Return to starting position.

6. Knee Slap

Alternate lifting the knees, touching each with both hands at the same time.

7. Leg Kicks

Alternating between legs, hop on one foot while kicking the other out in front.

8. Lunge

Stand with the feet together. Jump to the right, landing with the right foot extended forward and the left foot back. Return to the starting position, then jump immediately to the left, landing with the left foot extended forward and the right foot back. Extend arms overhead with each lunge.

9. Pendulum Swing

Swing legs side to side, hopping on one foot at a time.

10. Run/March in Place

Alternate lifting the knees, swinging the arms in opposition.

11. Stride Jump

Stand with one foot in front of the other. Jump up and switch feet, landing with the other foot in front.

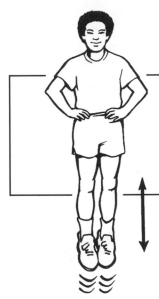

12. Superball

Bounce up and down on the balls of the feet. Let the heels touch the floor before bouncing back up.

Step Aerobics

There are 10 step aerobic exercises. The children need not learn these in any set order, nor do they need to learn them all at one time. Depending on the level of the children, teach them a few steps at a time, then add more as they progress.

1. Step Tap

Direction.   Facing the platform.

Procedure.   R foot tap, R foot down, L foot tap, L foot down.

Prompt.   Tap, step, tap, step (etc.).

2. Up/Down

Direction.   Facing the platform.

Procedure for R foot lead.   R foot up, L foot up, R foot down, L foot down. Procedure for L foot lead: L foot up, R foot up, L foot down, R foot down.

Prompt.   Up, up, down, down (etc.).

3. Tap Step

Direction. Facing the platform.

Procedure. R foot up, L foot up, R foot down, L foot tap down, L foot up, R foot up, L foot down, R foot tap down.

Prompt. Up, up, down, tap, up, up, down, tap (etc.). (Note: The tap step lets you switch from a R foot lead to a L foot lead in the up/down step.)

4. V Step

Direction. Facing the platform.

Procedure. R foot up (stepping to far right side of platform), L foot up (stepping to far left side of platform), R foot down (stepping back to center), L foot down (stepping back to center). Use a tap step to switch to a L foot lead.

Prompt. Up, up, down, down (etc.).

5. Lateral Step

Direction. Right side to platform (facing the end).

Procedure. R foot up (on right half of platform), L foot up (on left half of platform), R foot down (off right side), L foot down (off right side), L foot up (on left half of platform), R foot up (on right half of platform), L foot down (off left side), R foot down (off L side).

Prompt. Up, up, down, down (etc.).

6. Knee-Ups

Direction. Facing the platform.

Procedure. R foot up, L knee up, L foot down, R foot down, L foot up, R knee up, R foot down, L foot down.

Prompt. Up, lift, down, down (etc.).

7. Straddle Step

Direction.   Standing on top of platform facing the end.

Procedure.   R foot down (on right side), L foot down (on left side), R foot up, L foot up. Use a tap step on top to switch to a L foot lead.

Prompt.   Down, down, up, up (etc.).

8. Straddle Tap Step

Direction.   Standing on top of platform facing the end.

Procedure.   R foot down (on right side), L foot tap down (on left side), L foot up, R foot up, L foot down (on left side), R foot tap down (on right side), R foot up, L foot up.

Prompt.   Down, tap, up, up (etc.). (Note: A down means you execute another step with the other foot while supported on the down foot. A tap down means you tap your foot down then make the next step with the same foot.)

9. Straddle Knee-Ups

Direction.   Straddle platform facing one end.

Procedure.   R foot up, L knee up, L foot down, R foot down, L foot up, R knee up, R foot down, L foot down.

Prompt.   Up, lift, down, down (etc.).

10. Lunge

Direction.   Standing on top of platform facing one end.

Procedure.   R foot tap down and back, R foot up, L foot tap down and back, L foot up.

Prompt.   Tap, up, tap, up (etc.).

Muscular Strength and Endurance Exercises

The muscular strength and endurance activities in chapter 5 include exercises for various parts of the body. You will want to familiarize the children with these exercises before incorporating them into your activities. You will also find several activities with parachutes explained in this section.

Abdominal

There are six basic exercises presented next for developing the abdominal muscles. The children need not learn these in any set order, nor do they need to learn them all at one time. Depending on the level of the children, teach them a few exercises at a time, then add more as they progress.

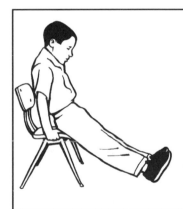

1. Chair Curl-Ups

Sit on the end of a chair, grasping the sides of the seat. Extend both legs straight out toward the floor. Slowly curl the knees into the chest, then extend legs back out to the starting position.

2. Crunches

Lie on your back with both knees up and hands behind the head. Tighten the abdomen and lift the shoulders off the floor, bringing elbows toward knees. Return to the starting position.

3. Curl-Down

Sit with knees bent and arms crossed on the chest. Slowly lower your back to the floor. Return to the starting position.

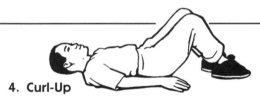

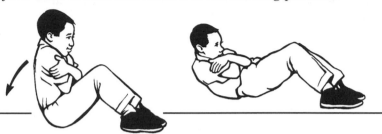

4. Curl-Up

Lie on your back with knees bent and arms extended toward the legs. Tighten the abdomen and lift shoulders off the floor as hands slide forward. Return to the starting position.

5. Reverse Curl-Up

Lie on your back with knees up and arms across the chest. Lift hips toward the ceiling while extending the legs. Return to the starting position.

6. Side Curl-Up

Lie on the side with knees bent. Place the bottom arm under the head and the top arm across the stomach. Lift the bottom shoulder off the floor with the top shoulder pointed toward the ceiling. Return to the starting position.

Upper Body

There are 10 basic exercises presented next for developing the muscles of the upper body. Some of these use simple equipment, including a foam ball or chairs. The children need not learn these in any set order, nor do they need to learn them all at one time. Depending on the level of the children, teach them a few exercises at a time, then add more as they progress.

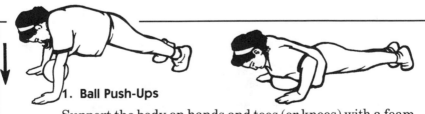

1. Ball Push-Ups

Support the body on hands and toes (or knees) with a foam ball positioned under the chest. Slowly lower the body onto the ball, pressing it down. Push up with arms and return to the starting position.

2. Bear Walk

Supporting the body on hands and feet, "walk" forward.

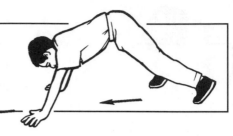

3. Chair Dips

Support the body on hands between two chairs. Keep the arms straight and legs extended out with heels on the floor. Slowly lower the buttocks toward the floor by bending at the elbow. Return to the starting position. Make sure the chairs are secure (you can place the back legs of the chair against a wall).

4. Chair Push-Ups

Support the body on hands between two chairs and extend legs to the back. Slowly lower the chest between the chairs by bending at the elbows. Straighten the arms and return to the starting position.

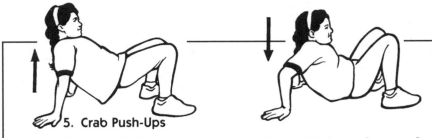

5. Crab Push-Ups

Support the body on hands and feet, with knees bent and arms straight. Bend the elbows and lower the buttocks toward the floor. Straighten the arms and return to starting position.

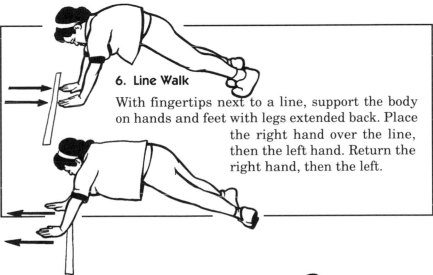

6. Line Walk

With fingertips next to a line, support the body on hands and feet with legs extended back. Place the right hand over the line, then the left hand. Return the right hand, then the left.

7. Partner Pull-Up

Lie on your back between the legs of a partner. Grasping the partner's hands, pull your body up off the floor. The partner should keep a straight back and the knees slightly bent; the partner does not pull up. Lower your body to the starting position.

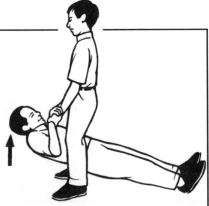

8. Push-Ups

Support the body on hands and feet (or knees) with legs extended back and arms straight. Slowly bend the elbows and lower the chest toward the floor. Straighten the arms and return to the starting position.

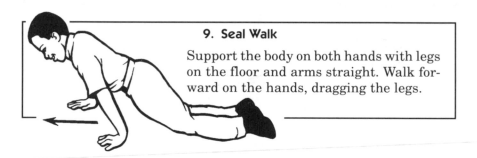

9. Seal Walk

Support the body on both hands with legs on the floor and arms straight. Walk forward on the hands, dragging the legs.

10. Wall Push-Ups

Stand one or two steps back from a wall. Face the wall and lean against it, supporting the body on both hands with arms straight. Slowly bend the elbows and bring the chest toward the wall. Straighten the arms and return to the starting position.

Lower Body

There are 15 basic exercises presented next for developing muscles of the lower body, or legs. The children need not learn these in any set order, nor do they need to learn them all at one time. Depending on the level of the children, teach them a few exercises at a time, then add more as they progress.

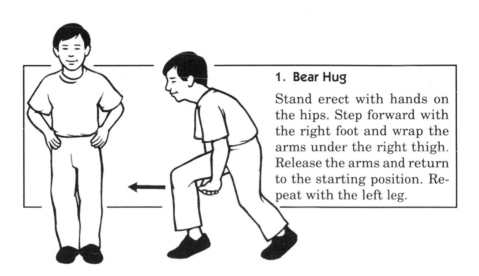

1. Bear Hug

Stand erect with hands on the hips. Step forward with the right foot and wrap the arms under the right thigh. Release the arms and return to the starting position. Repeat with the left leg.

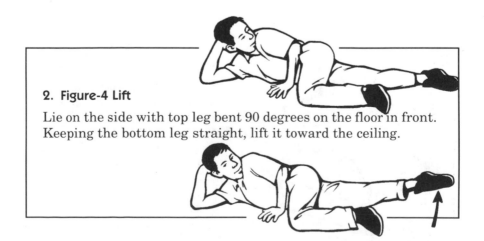

2. Figure-4 Lift

Lie on the side with top leg bent 90 degrees on the floor in front. Keeping the bottom leg straight, lift it toward the ceiling.

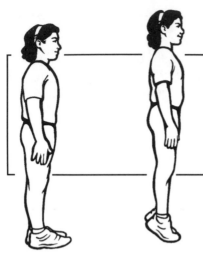

3. Heel Lifts

Stand erect with feet several inches apart and arms at sides. Lift the heels off the floor to stand on the balls of the feet. Lower the heels and repeat.

4. Hip Abduction

Lie on the side with hips and knees bent. Slowly lift the top leg up until the knee is above the hip. Lower the leg to starting position and repeat.

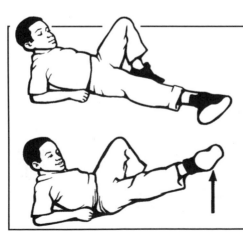

5. Hip Adduction

Recline on the floor with upper body resting on elbows. Bend one leg, keeping foot flat on the floor. Keep the other leg straight with the foot turned parallel to the floor. Lift the straight leg up 10 to 12 inches, then lower it to the floor. Return to the starting position and repeat.

6. Hip Extension

Stand one or two steps back from a wall. Face the wall and lean against it, supporting the body with both hands. Slowly lift one leg in back while squeezing the buttocks. Return to the starting position and repeat.

7. Hip Flexion

Stand erect with hands on hips. Slowly lift one knee in front. Lower the leg, touching the floor with toe. Repeat. (For better balance, rest the opposite hand against a wall.)

8. Knee Dips

Stand erect with hands on hips and one foot in front of the other (about one step). Bend the back knee and slowly lower it toward the floor. Just before touching the floor, push up with the front leg and return to the starting position. Alternate legs with each dip by switching feet, or do continuous dips on one leg before switching to the other. Stay erect and keep your back straight.

9. Leg Curl

Rest on hands (or elbows) and knees with one leg extended back, parallel to the floor. Slowly bend the knee, bringing the foot toward the buttocks. Extend the leg outward slowly and repeat. To avoid arching the back, do not bring the leg up past parallel.

10. Leg Extension

Recline on the floor with upper body resting on elbows. Keep legs bent, with one foot flat on the floor and the other held 1 to 2 inches in the air. Slowly straighten the foot held off the ground, bringing it toward the ceiling. Return to the starting position and repeat.

11. Side Leg Lift

Lie on the side with one leg on top of the other, keeping hips one on top of the other as well. Slowly lift the top leg 8 to 10 inches. Lower the leg, returning to the starting position, and repeat. Avoid banging legs together on the return.

12. Squats

Stand erect with hands on hips and feet shoulder-width apart. Slowly bend the knees, lowering the buttocks toward the floor (as if sitting in a chair). Do not let the knees bend past 90 degrees. Straighten the legs and return to the starting position. The back should remain straight during the entire exercise, and the thighs should never go past being parallel with the floor.

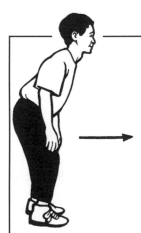

13. Standing Long Jump

Stand with arms at sides and feet slightly apart. Bend at the knees and hips, swinging arms backward. As arms come forward, jump outward as far as possible. Land on both feet in a balanced position. Turn around and repeat in the other direction.

14. Vertical Jump

Stand with arms at sides and feet slightly apart. Bend at the knees and hips, swinging arms backward. As arms come forward, jump up as high as possible, bringing arms up overhead. Land on both feet in a balanced position and repeat.

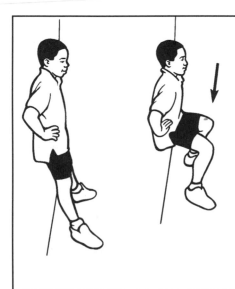

15. Wall Squats

Stand erect with hands on hips, back against a wall, and feet shoulder-width apart. Keeping back against wall, slowly bend knees, lowering buttocks toward the floor (as if sitting in a chair). Do not let the knees bend past 90 degrees. Straighten the legs and return to the starting position. Your back should remain against the wall during the entire exercise, and thighs should never go past being parallel to the floor.

Resistance Exercises

The following eight exercises use resistance to develop muscles of the upper and lower body. The children need not learn these in any set order, nor do they need to learn them all at one time. Depending on the level of the children, teach them a few exercises at a time, then add more as they progress.

(Do the following exercises while holding dumbbells or balls.)

1. Bent-Over Rowing

Stand with feet shoulder-width apart. Bend at the waist until back is almost parallel to the floor (back should be straight). Extend the arms toward floor. Slowly lift the arms by pulling the elbows up toward the ceiling. Once elbows are above the back, lower the arms and repeat.

2. Biceps Curl

Stand erect with feet shoulder-width apart and arms extended down at sides. Keeping elbows close to the body, bend them and lift hands toward the chest. Slowly lower hands and repeat.

3. Lateral Deltoid Lift

Stand erect with feet shoulder-width apart and arms extended down at sides. Slowly lift arms out to the sides until parallel to the floor. Pause at the top, then lower to the starting position. Keep elbows slightly bent during the exercise.

4. Overhead Press

Stand erect with feet shoulder-width apart and elbows bent with hands at shoulders. Slowly straighten arms, lifting hands overhead. Lower to the starting position and repeat.

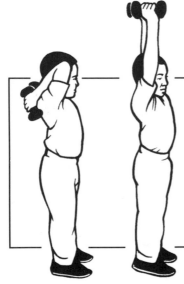

5. Overhead Triceps Extension

Stand erect with feet shoulder-width apart. Put hands together behind the head so that elbows are pointed toward the ceiling. Slowly straighten the arms, extending hands up overhead. Lower the hands to the starting position and repeat.

6. Shoulder Shrugs

Stand erect with feet shoulder-width apart and arms extended down at sides. Slowly lift shoulders toward the ears, pause, then return to the starting position.

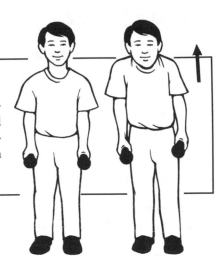

7. Single-Arm Rowing

Holding a weight in one hand only, stand with the opposite foot in front. Bend at the waist and place the empty hand on the forward knee, extending the other arm toward the floor. Slowly lift the weight by pulling the elbow up toward the ceiling. Once the elbow is above your back, lower the arm and repeat.

8. Upright Rowing

Stand erect with feet shoulder-width apart and arms extended down toward floor in front, weights held end to end. Keeping hands together, pull elbows up toward ceiling. Once hands reach the chin, lower the arms and repeat.

Parachute Exercises

The children use a parachute to do the following six exercises, which not only develop muscular strength and endurance, but also offer a fun group activity. The children need not learn these in any set order, nor do they need to learn them all at one time. Depending on the level of the children, teach them a few exercises at a time, then add more as they progress.

1. Seated Facing the Parachute

Biceps curl.   Grasp the parachute with arms straight and palms facing up. Bend at the elbows, pulling the parachute toward the chin.

Rowing.   Grasp the parachute with arms straight and palms facing down. Pull the parachute toward the stomach.

Front deltoid lift.   Grasp the parachute with arms straight and palms facing down. Keep the arms straight and lift the parachute overhead.

2. Seated with Back to Parachute

Overhead triceps extension.   Grasp the parachute behind the neck with elbows bent and palms facing up. Straighten the arms, lifting the parachute overhead.

3. Standing Facing Parachute

Biceps curl.   Grasp the parachute with arms straight and palms facing forward. Bend at the elbow, pulling the parachute up toward the chin.

Upright rowing.   Grasp the parachute with arms straight, hands close together, and palms facing the body. Pull the parachute up toward the chin, bringing elbows up and out.

Front deltoid lift.   Grasp the parachute with arms straight and palms facing body. Keep the arms straight and lift the parachute overhead.

4. Standing with Back to Parachute

Overhead triceps extension. Grasp the parachute behind the neck with elbows bent and palms facing up. Straighten the arms, lifting the parachute overhead.

5. Standing with Right Side to Parachute

Lateral deltoid lift (right arm). Grasp the parachute with right arm straight and palm facing body. Keep the arm straight and lift until it is parallel to the ground.

6. Standing with Left Side to Parachute

Lateral deltoid lift (left arm). Grasp the parachute with left arm straight and palm facing body. Keep the arm straight and lift until it is parallel to the ground.

Flexibility Exercises

No doubt you have noticed that even young children show dramatic differences in flexibility. Because of these differences it is important to incorporate flexibility into your program. The exercises in this section focus on two types of flexibility, dynamic and static, to help children at all levels improve. You will want to teach the children how to safely perform these exercises before incorporating them into your activities.

Dynamic Stretches

The eight dynamic stretches described here allow children to move in a controlled manner while developing flexibility. The children need not learn these in any set order, nor do they need to learn them all at one time. Depending on the level of the children, teach them a few stretches at a time, then add more as they progress.

1. Backward Arm Circles

Stand erect with feet shoulder-width apart and arms extended to the sides, parallel to the floor. Slowly circle the arms backward. Start with small circles, then move to large ones.

2. Body Circle

Stand with feet shoulder-width apart, knees slightly bent, and arms extended overhead. Slowly lean to the side and bring arms toward the floor, while bending at the waist. Continue with hands moving across the floor to the other side, then upward to the starting position. Repeat by going in the opposite direction.

3. Lateral Trunk Flexion

Stand erect with hands on hips, feet shoulder-width apart, and knees slightly bent. Bending at the waist, lean to the side, return to straight position, then lean to the other side. Repeat, moving side to side.

4. Leg Lifts

Stand alongside a wall, resting a hand on it. Slowly lift the outside leg in front, lower it, then lift it in back. Continue moving the leg forward and backward. Control the momentum of the leg swing.

5. Neck Stretches

Stretch A: Stand erect with feet shoulder-width apart and hands on hips. Keeping the chin up, look toward the right, pause, and look to the left. Pause each time and repeat, looking side to side.

Stretch B: Stand erect with feet shoulder-width apart and hands on hips. Lower the right ear toward the right shoulder, pause, then lower the left ear toward the left shoulder. Pause each time and repeat, tilting head side to side.

6. Overhead Reach

Stand with feet shoulder-width apart and knees slightly bent. Place one hand on hip and lean to the side, extending the opposite arm overhead. After a short pause, lean to the other side, extending the other arm overhead. Repeat, moving from side to side.

7. Seated Trunk Rotation

Sit on the floor with legs extended in front and feet together. Reach to the side and touch the floor with both hands. Slowly twist the other direction and touch the floor on the other side. Continue twisting from side to side.

8. Shoulder Rolls

Stand erect with feet shoulder-width apart and arms extended down at sides. Slowly raise the shoulders toward the ears, then rotate them backward and down to the starting position. Continue in circles. Switch to a forward direction after the desired repetitions are complete.

Static Stretches

The 14 static stretches described here require the children to briefly hold a stretched muscle for at least 10 seconds. The actual length of time depends on the children's experience with stretching and their maturity. Immature or less experienced children have a hard time engaging in static stretches for more than 10 seconds at a time. The children need not learn these in any set order, nor do they need to learn them all at one time. Depending on the level of the children, teach them a few stretches at a time, then add more as they progress.

1. Butterfly

Sit on the floor with soles of the feet touching and heels pulled in toward body. Grab the toes and slowly lower the knees toward the floor. Hold.

2. Crossed-Leg Stretch

Sit on the floor with legs crossed (Indian-style). Slowly lean forward, extending the arms out on the floor as far as possible. Hold.

3. Hip Flexor

Stand with one foot in front of the other, toes pointed forward. Bend the front knee 90 degrees and extend the rear leg back, lowering the hips toward the floor. Hold. (Keep the front knee even with or behind the front ankle.)

4. Knee to Chest

Lying on your back, grasp one leg under the knee and pull it to the chest. Keep the other knee slightly bent and foot on the floor. Hold. Repeat with the other leg, then with both legs at once.

5. Lateral Oblique

Stand alongside a wall, one or two steps away. Place the forearm on the wall with elbow bent 90 degrees and hand pointed toward ceiling. Slowly lean hips toward the wall and hold. Repeat on the other side.

6. Seated Hip Stretch

Sit with one leg straight and the other bent, crossed over the straight leg. Twist to the side of the bent leg and place the opposite elbow outside the bent knee. Hold. Switch legs and repeat on the other side.

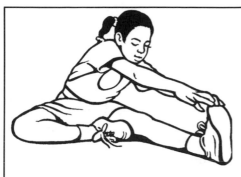

7. Seated L

Sit on the floor with one leg straight and the other bent, with foot against the inside of the straight leg. Reach both hands toward the foot or ankle of the straight leg. Hold. Switch legs and repeat on the other side.

8. Seated Quadriceps Stretch

Sitting on the floor, lean to one side, keeping the leg bent. Grasp the other foot at the shoelaces and pull it back, keeping it off the floor (rest on the opposite hand for balance). Hold. Switch legs and repeat on the other side.

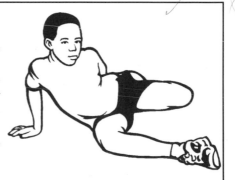

9. Seated Straddle

Sit on the floor with legs spread. Reach with both hands toward one foot or ankle. Hold, then reach with both hands toward the other foot or ankle. Hold.

10. Seated Toe Touch

Sit on the floor with legs straight ahead (it is best not to lock the knees) and feet together. With both hands, slowly reach out toward both feet or ankles. Hold.

11. Standing Quadriceps Stretch

Stand one or two steps from a wall and place a hand on it. Grasp the opposite foot with the free hand and pull the heel toward the buttocks. Hold. Switch legs and repeat on the other side.

12. Static Overhead Reach

Stand with feet shoulder-width apart and knees slightly bent. Place one hand on hip and lean to that side. Extend the opposite arm overhead and hold. Switch sides and repeat.

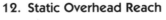

13. Triceps Stretch

Stand erect with feet shoulder-width apart. Lift one arm overhead, bending it at the elbow. Grasp the elbow with the opposite hand and pull slightly. Hold. Switch arms and repeat on the other side.

14. Wall Calf Stretch

Stand one or two steps from a wall, with one foot in front of the other and both hands on the wall. Keeping the back heel on the floor, bend the front knee and lean toward the wall. Hold. Switch legs and repeat with the other heel on the floor.

Part Two

Fitness Activities

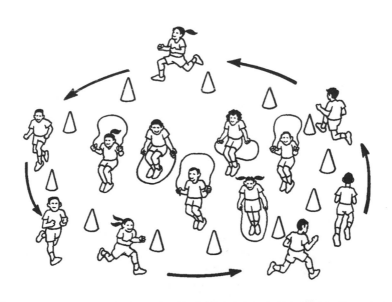

Cardiorespiratory Endurance

The 27 activities in this chapter will help you improve children's cardiorespiratory endurance while teaching important components and principles of fitness. Most of the activities can be adapted to an array of ability levels, ranging from kindergarten through sixth grade, simply by varying the duration, intensity, or time to meet the particular needs of the children. Several activities require knowing how to perform certain exercises, which are described in chapter 3. Several activities require you to make circuit cards or task cards; information and suggestions on making the cards are in the appendix.

The amount of time you spend in an activity depends largely on the children's ability. As I mentioned in chapter 2, I recommend you involve children in fitness-related activities for about 25% of the time you spend with them. You may choose to use one activity as a complete cardiorespiratory workout or to combine two or three activities to achieve your objective. Whichever approach you choose, you'll find that these activities, when done correctly, help elevate children's heart rates.

Before beginning an activity, briefly discuss its purpose. Explain and use key components and principles of fitness, such as cardiorespiratory endurance, overload, intensity, and heart rate. While the children are doing the activity, include specific comments and questions about what is taking place and how it relates to fitness. For example, ask the children what they think their hearts are doing. When you're done with the activity, take a few moments to answer any questions or to discuss how the children feel about the activity and what their bodies have experienced. This broadens their knowledge of fitness while giving them hands-on opportunities to experience exactly what you have taught them.

 Aerobic Dance Circuit

Grades: 3-6

Before You Begin

Teach the children the 12 basic aerobic dance steps (see chapter 3); explain the terms *aerobic* and *circuit training*; make aerobic dance circuit cards (see the appendix to find out how to make cards).

Equipment

Music; 12 aerobic dance circuit cards; 12 cones.

Organization

Place children in groups of two to four. Arrange cones in a large circle or oval, with a circuit card on each cone.

Procedure

Place one group of children at each station. When you begin the music, each group performs the step written on their card. On a signal (a break in the music or a whistle) they rotate counterclockwise to the next station and begin performing the next step. Continue until the circuit is completed.

Variation

Once children become proficient at performing the 12 basic steps they can move on to combinations. Start with 2 steps written on one card (for example, jumping jacks and knee slap). The children perform both steps, switching from one to the other every 4, 8, or 16 counts. You can increase the number of steps in a combination as the children's ability increases.

Teaching Tips

Rotate the children about every 30 seconds. Remind them to move quickly to the next station and begin immediately.

Specify several stations as low impact (no bouncing up and down). Alternate the low-impact and high-impact stations.

You will need music with approximately 140 to 155 beats per minute. Although many children will not accurately exercise to the beat, the upbeat tempo will keep them motivated. (If you are unsure how to determine beats per minute, see p. 154 in the appendix.)

Homework Suggestion

Assign three to six of the aerobic dance steps learned in class to be practiced at home.

 2 ▸ Aerobic Task Card
Grades: 3-6

Before You Begin

Teach the children the 12 basic aerobic dance steps (see chapter 3); explain the term *aerobic*; make aerobic task cards (see the appendix for instructions; Figure 4.1 shows a sample).

Equipment

Music; 8 to 15 aerobic task cards; cones.

Organization

Place the children in small groups of two or three. Give each group a task card. Set up cones in an oval in the center of the area (about 50-75 feet long and 30-40 feet wide).

─── Aerobic Task Card ───

Directions: Perform the following exercises and movements.
Return this card to the teacher when you are finished.

1. Jog 2 laps around the cones.
2. Do 12 knee slaps.
3. Skip 1 lap around the cones.
4. Do 10 jumping jacks.
5. Do 20 downhill skiers.
6. Gallop 2 laps around the cones.
7. Do 8 leg kicks.
8. Jog 3 laps around the cones.
9. Do 18 stride jumps.
10. Walk 2 laps around the cones.

Figure 4.1   A sample aerobic task card.

Procedure

When the music begins the groups perform in order the activities listed on their cards. When they finish they return the card to you. If time permits they may select another card and start again.

Variation

If the children are good readers they can do this activity individually instead of in groups.

Teaching Tips

When selecting groups try to place below-level readers with above-level readers.

When making task cards, vary the order of the exercises so each group is working on a different one.

End each task card with a slower activity, such as walking.

Choose music speed depending on children's ability. You will need music that is about 140 to 155 beats per minute. Although many children will not accurately perform the exercises to the beat, the upbeat tempo keeps them motivated. (If you are unsure how to determine beats per minute, see p. 154 in the appendix.)

Safety Tips

Because many groups will be moving randomly around the area, remind children to move with caution. Perform all locomotor movements in the same direction.

Homework Suggestion

Have children make their own aerobic task cards. They practice the exercises on their cards at home, then bring them to the next physical education class.

3 ▸ Around the Block

Grades: K-3

Before You Begin

Review basic locomotor skills, such as walking, jogging, skipping, and galloping; make cards for the cones (see the appendix).

Equipment

Music; 4 cones with a card on each one.

Organization

Place cones in a square about 30 feet on a side (see Figure 4.2). On each cone put a card with a different locomotor movement, such as jogging, galloping, or skipping. Scatter children around the outside of the square.

Procedure

When the music begins the children move counterclockwise around the cones, performing the locomotor movement on the card at the last cone they passed. As shown in Figure 4.2, where the children are on the "block" determines how they are moving. Once they reach the next corner they read the card and change movements. On the signal (a break in the music or a whistle) the children change directions and begin moving clockwise around the block.

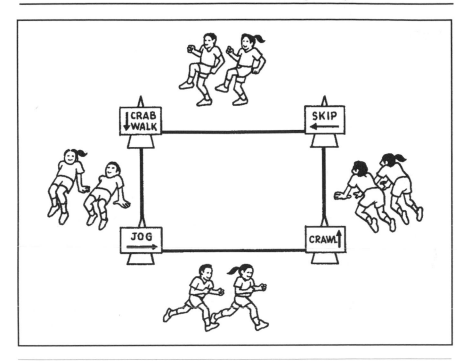

Figure 4.2   Children participating in Around the Block.

Variations

Locomotor movements can be done forward when moving counterclockwise and backward when moving clockwise.

Two different locomotor movements can be written on each card, one for moving in each direction.

Muscular strength and endurance exercises can be added to the activity in three ways:

1. Each time the signal is given to change direction, students perform a teacher-designated exercise (e.g., push-ups) before going on.
2. On each card you write an exercise and the number of repetitions, along with the locomotor movement. Children perform the exercise at each corner.
3. Place a pile of exercise cards at each cone. When children arrive at the cone they take a card from the pile, perform the exercise, and return the card to the bottom of the pile.

Keep in mind that using exercises in this activity may decrease the continuous cardiovascular benefit if children have to wait to perform them. However, if you set up the activity properly, vigorous cardiorespiratory exercise can be sustained.

Safety Tip

To avoid collisions, make a rule that to pass someone while going around the block you must move on the outside.

Homework Suggestion

Have children perform Around the Block at home around their own block or through the neighborhood, using different locomotor movements to travel.

4 ▶ Cardio Circuit

Grades: 3-6

Before You Begin

Teach children the basic step-aerobic steps (shown in chapter 3); they will also need to know how to jump rope and perform spot jumping (see Activity #26 for more information); make 12 circuit cards (see the appendix).

Equipment

Music; 12 cones; 9 aerobic step benches; 12 circuit cards (3 step aerobics, 3 rope jumping, 3 spot jumping, and 3 jogging); 9 jump ropes; 9 poly spots. You want all children to have their own equipment, so the pieces needed depend on the size of the group. I have suggested 9 of each piece, which will accommodate between 25 and 35 children.

Organization

Set up the cones in a circle or oval, leaving enough space around the outside for children to jog without interfering with others. Place one circuit card on each cone, distributing the cards in sequence so that the same activity is repeated every fourth station. The children are placed in groups of two or three at each station, and equipment is divided equally among the corresponding stations. (This setup is shown in Figure 4.3.)

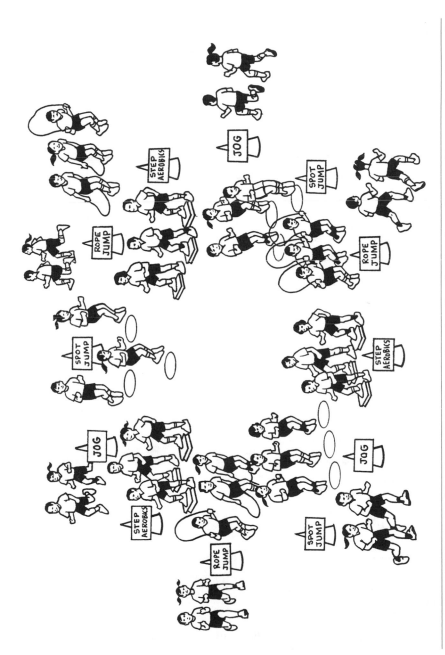

Figure 4.3   Children participating in a cardiovascular circuit using jogging, step aerobics, rope jumping, and spot jumping.

Procedure

When you begin the music, the children perform the activity written on their circuit cards. At a signal (a break in the music or a whistle) they rotate counterclockwise to the next station and begin the next activity. Continue the procedure for 8 to 12 minutes.

Teaching Tips

If enough of the prescribed equipment is not available, substitute an aerobic dance exercise (different from step-aerobic steps; they are also shown in chapter 3). The joggers run around the perimeter of all the stations.

Safety Tip

Children should move with caution when switching stations because joggers may still be running and rope jumpers still turning their ropes.

Homework Suggestion

Have children design and implement their own cardiovascular circuit at home. A sample circuit could include jogging, riding a bike, jumping rope, walking, and doing jumping jacks. Children draw pictures or write descriptions of their circuits and bring them to the next physical education class.

5 ▸ Circle Drills

Grades: 2-6

Before You Begin

Review basic locomotor skills, such as skipping, jogging, galloping, walking, and hopping.

Equipment

Music or a tambourine; 1 jump rope and 1 hoop for each child.

Organization

Place children in a large circle. Put a hoop with a jump rope inside of it inside the circle next to each child.

Procedure

When the music (or tambourine) begins the children perform a locomotor movement clockwise around the circle. On a signal (a break in the music or a whistle) each child stops in front of the nearest hoop, picks up the hoop or the rope, and quickly begins either jumping rope or jumping in and out of the hoop (after laying it back on the floor). The children continue to jump until the next signal, when they return the hoop or rope to its original place and begin another locomotor movement, this time counterclockwise. The activity continues in this pattern until the allotted time has elapsed.

Variations

If space permits, use two or three circles with fewer children in each one.

Let the children use the hoops as jump ropes instead of laying them on the floor for jumping.

Designate several locomotor movements that can be performed and let children choose among them.

Let the children be creative with their movements around the circle.

Teaching Tips

Allow the children to choose between the rope and hoop on their own. This offers an alternative for those who are not skillful rope jumpers.

Use the time when children are moving around the circle to assess locomotor skills.

To avoid arguments over who got to which hoop or rope first, make a rule that two children cannot touch the same object at the same time—or let them share!

Safety Tips

Remind children to stay in place and face the center of the circle when turning the rope or hoop for jumping. Caution children to stay outside of the circle when performing the locomotor movements so they do not trip over the hoops and ropes.

Homework Suggestion

Have children practice alternating between jumping and jogging at home.

6 Crazy Cones
Grades: K-3

Before You Begin

Let the children practice moving safely through general space.

Equipment

Music; as many cones as possible, preferably at least one for each child.

Organization

Scatter cones around the area, with half standing and half lying down. Divide the children into two groups and scatter them around the area.

Procedure

When the music begins, Group A tries to knock down all cones that are standing, while Group B tries to stand up all cones that are lying down. After 30 to 45 seconds the groups switch roles. The activity continues with the roles of the groups continually switching.

Variations

All children form one group and attempt to knock down or stand up all of the cones in a certain amount of time. Keep track of the time and see if the group can improve. Give the children alternative ways to knock down or stand up the cones (with their feet, heads, elbows, knees, etc.).

Teaching Tips

Although there are two teams, the object is not to determine a winner or loser. Avoid focusing on the status of the cones; instead, keep the activity moving.

This is an activity of relatively short duration. You may want to use it as a warm-up or combine it with another cardiorespiratory activity.

If you do not have cones, use empty 2-liter plastic bottles or paper cups.

Safety Tips

Caution the children to watch out for others while moving through general space. Watch for children who may kick or knock cones over violently.

Homework Suggestion

Have the children collect empty 2-liter plastic bottles and play Crazy Cones at home with their family or friends.

7 Crazy Sprints
Grades: K-3

Before You Begin

Review basic locomotor skills, such as skipping, jogging, and galloping.

Equipment

None.

Organization

Divide the children into two groups; have them stand at one end of a playing area 20 to 40 yards long.

Procedure

On a signal to begin, the children in Group A run to the other end of the area. Group B follows on the next signal, which is given when Group A reaches the halfway point. Before each turn you give the groups a stunt to perform at the halfway point. Upon reaching halfway, each child performs the stunt.

Try directing students to do stunts like these:

1. Touch the floor with your hands [elbows, knees, stomach, back, etc.].
2. Spin around 1 time [2 times, etc.].
3. Jump into the air.
4. Perform an exercise [e.g., jumping jacks].
5. Touch your knees with your hands.
6. Duck under a low bridge.
7. Jump over a creek [canyon, river, etc.].

Variation

Instead of having students do stunts only in the middle, mark off two or three locations with cones and have the children do a stunt at each one.

Teaching Tips

Give the groups names, such as roadrunners, rockets, or blazers. Call out the group's name as a signal to begin running. This adds more excitement to the activity.

As soon as Group B finishes, start Group A back in the other direction with a new stunt.

Safety Tip

Caution Group B not to run into Group A, who have already finished.

Homework Suggestion

Have children try Crazy Sprints at home using objects in their yard or a nearby park as markers to perform a stunt. (For example, run to a tree and hop around it; run to a wall and jump up and touch as high on the wall as possible.)

8   Distance Running and Walking
Grades: 3-6

Before You Begin

Discuss *duration* and *intensity* as they relate to distance running; review graphing skills.

Equipment

Cones (optional; use them if you need to mark off a running area); graph paper; pencils or colored markers.

Organization

Determine a running course around the grounds, preferably 1/8 to 1/4 mile. Scatter the children around the course.

Procedure

The children run or walk around the course at their own pace for the time you have allotted. This time should start at around 4 to 6 minutes and go up to 10 to 12 minutes as children improve their cardiorespiratory endurance. The children keep track of the number of laps they complete around the course and fill in their individual graphs.

Teaching Tips

Let children move in small groups and talk with each other.

To help in keeping track of laps, give children rubber bands to wear on their wrist, one every time they complete a lap.

Vary the allotted time with the ability of the children.

Spreading children around the course at the start helps keep the slower children from being obvious. It makes it difficult, however, to hand out rubber bands for laps completed because everyone started at a different location.

You can use this activity to periodically assess fitness levels by tracking progress on the graph.

Use the graphs only to track individual progress; do not post them, which can embarrass some children and encourage others to be dishonest about their laps. A sample graph is shown in Figure 4.4.

Safety Tip

Make a rule that when passing someone on the course you must pass on the right.

Homework Suggestion

Have children create a course at home and run it. They can keep track of how many laps they complete, graph the results, and bring them in to show you.

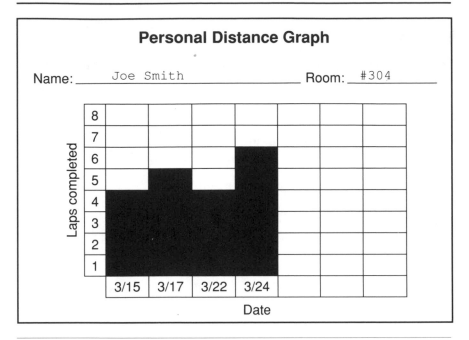

Personal Distance Graph

Name: _____Joe Smith_____   Room: __#304__

Figure 4.4 A bar graph showing the number of laps a child completed in four different class periods.

9 Flip-Flop

Grades: K-3

Before You Begin

Let children practice moving safely through general space.

Equipment

Music or tambourine.

Organization

Scatter the children around the area in a large oval.

Procedure

The children jog around the oval in one direction. Every 15 to 30 seconds when a signal is given, the children all drop, touch their stomachs to the ground, flip over, touch their backs to the ground, then get up and begin jogging in the opposite direction.

Variations

Instead of jogging, students use different locomotor movements to move around the oval. To help develop muscular strength and endurance children do an exercise (e.g., push-ups, sit-ups) each time they flip-flop.

Teaching Tips

This is an activity of relatively short duration. You may want to use it as a warm-up activity or combine it with another cardiorespiratory activity. Children enjoy having everyone yell "Flip-flop!" as they go down to the ground.

Safety Tips

Caution students to stay under control while flopping and flipping so they don't kick anyone.

Before beginning have the children practice jogging and falling to the ground several times.

Caution students who get up quickly to watch where they are running so they don't collide with those still on the ground.

Homework Suggestion

Have the children practice Flip-Flop at home by running in place and dropping to the floor.

10 Four, Three, Two, One
Grades: 3-6

Before You Begin

Explain the term *interval training*.

Equipment

4 cones or bases.

Organization

Mark off a square about 60 feet on a side and place a cone (or base) at each corner. Divide the class into four groups and place one group at each corner. (It is best not to have more than eight in a group.)

Procedure

On the signal to begin each group runs counterclockwise to the next cone. After reaching it the group walks to the next cone, where they wait until you give the next signal to begin. This sequence is repeated four times. Then the group runs the distance of two cones 3 times, three cones 2 times, and four cones 1 time. Between the running intervals the group walks a distance equal to the previous run. If more intensity is needed, have the children jog instead of walking.

Variations

Do the sequence backward (1, 2, 3, 4). Use other shapes (triangle, octagon, etc.) or have several squares.

Teaching Tips

Remind the children that they are not racing. With large classes use more than four corners.

Safety Tip

Caution the children to be careful when passing others. Passing should be done on the outside.

Homework Suggestion

Using empty 2-liter plastic bottles, have the children set up their own courses at home and practice running the intervals.

11 Frizz-B Fren-Z

Grades: 2-6

Before You Begin

Let the children practice moving safely through general space.

Equipment

1 foam flying disk for every two children (foam disks are available from most sporting goods suppliers; a foam ball or soft object can be substituted); cones to mark off boundaries.

Organization

Scatter children around the area in groups of two. Each pair has a foam disk.

Procedure

Each pair plays a game of tag using the flying disk. To begin, one partner is selected to be It, and the other partner is given 5 seconds to run away, making sure to stay in the boundaries. Once the 5 seconds are counted, It attempts to catch the other partner by tagging with the disk or throwing the disk to make contact. Once the partner is caught, the roles are reversed and the game continues. When a disk is thrown out-of-bounds, the partner being chased must run in place until It retrieves the disk and returns inside the boundaries.

Variation

Play the game with three players; two are It. The person holding the disk cannot move while touching it, so the two Its must pass the disk back and forth as they try to get close to the person they are chasing. After the partner is caught players rotate so that each gets a chance to be chased.

Teaching Tips

Mark each disk with a number to help avoid confusion or arguments over the disks. If throwing objects at people is not acceptable in your program, then play this activity solely as a tag game.

Safety Tips

Because all of the children are playing simultaneously in one area, it's important that you caution them to watch out for others! Playing this game outside in a large area helps avoid collisions.

Homework Suggestion

Have the children play at home with family or friends using homemade balls made out of newspaper and masking tape.

12 ▸ Grass Drills
Grades: 3-6

Before You Begin

Discuss proper pacing techniques; let children practice jogging in a small group, with the objective being to jog at the same pace and stay close together; practice jogging and falling to the ground in a safe, controlled manner.

Equipment

Whistle.

Organization

Divide children into groups of three and scatter the groups around the area.

Procedure

Each group begins by jogging around the area in a single-file line. On a signal (whistle), the child at the end of the line drops and touches her or his stomach to the ground. The other two members continue jogging, and the "dropper" jumps up and runs quickly to get to the front of the line. On the next signal the next child at the end of the line drops to the ground. The activity continues with each group member getting numerous opportunities to drop to the ground.

Variation

Instead of returning to the same group, the child who dropped can run to the front of a different group.

Teaching Tips

Remind groups to jog at one continuous, moderate pace. (If they jog too fast the child who dropped to the ground will have a difficult time catching them.) Use a large open area to give groups freedom to move.

Safety Tips

Remind the children to drop to the ground softly to avoid injury. Use a surface that is conducive to falling. Caution the children to watch out for other groups while moving throughout the area.

Homework Suggestion

Grass Drills can be practiced at home with family members. Everyone jogs in place, with one person acting as the leader. When the leader calls out a name, that person drops to the floor, then gets up and continues jogging.

13 Hurdles

Grades: K-3

Before You Begin

Let the children practice moving safely through general space.

Equipment

Music; 20 to 30 hurdles (preferably one for each child); cones of varying heights (6-18 inches).

Note: Plastic hurdles that insert into a cone are recommended for this activity; they are available from most sporting goods suppliers. Other homemade versions can be used, however, such as yarn stretched between two cones, a plastic wand or hockey stick laid across two cones, several cones placed side by side, or tape on the floor.

Organization

Scatter hurdles and children around the area.

Procedure

This is an interval training activity. When you begin the music the children begin to run, jumping over as many hurdles as possible and keeping count of how many they clear. After 30 seconds stop the music for the children to walk for 30 seconds. When the music begins again the children get another 30 seconds to jump over hurdles, trying to clear more than the previous time. Continue the activity for the time available, with the children trying to improve their accomplishments during each 30-second interval.

Variations

Try this activity having the children go under the hurdles instead of over them. Have the children follow partners. Give the children objects to carry in their hands as they run (footballs, foam balls, etc.).

Teaching Tips

Use hurdles of different heights so that every child can be successful and at the same time challenged. If some children in your group have trouble jumping into the air, use tape on the floor as the hurdle.

Do not focus on comparing between jumpers how many hurdles they cleared in the 30 seconds. Focus instead on improvement.

Have the children pick up any hurdles they knock over.

To help improve their aerobic fitness remind children to move at a pace that will let them continue the activity for its allotted time. This is an activity of short duration. You may want to use it as a warm-up or combine it with another cardiorespiratory activity.

The rest-to-work ratio should be kept at 1:1.

Safety Tip

Caution children to watch out for others as they move through general space.

Homework Suggestion

Have children set up their own hurdles in their backyards or at a nearby park. Many objects around the home can be used as hurdles, such as plastic buckets, piles of leaves, or paper bags with stones or dirt in them to hold them in place.

14 ▶ In, Out, and Around
Grades: K-3

Before You Begin

Review basic locomotor skills, such as skipping, jogging, and galloping; let the children practice moving safely through general space.

Equipment

Music; whistle; 1 hoop for each child.

Organization

Scatter the hoops around the area on the floor. Scatter children throughout the hoops.

Procedure

Determine three signals at the beginning, such as these:

- One short whistle — move throughout the area.
- Two short whistles — jump in and out of a hoop.
- Three short whistles — run around the outside of a hoop.

When you begin the music the children perform a locomotor movement around the area without touching the hoops. When you sound two short whistles each child quickly finds a hoop and begins jumping in and out on both feet. When you sound one short whistle the children begin moving throughout the area again. When you sound three short whistles the children find hoops and run around the outside of the hoop until you sound one short whistle again. Continue the activity using alternating whistle commands.

Variations

Instead of having different commands to follow, let the children choose whether they want to jump in and out of the hoop or run around the outside.

Use signs, like raising your hand, as commands so that the children have to look for instructions instead of listening (you will need to be centrally located so all children can see you easily).

Teaching Tips

This is an activity of relatively short duration. You may want to use it as a warm-up or combine it with another cardiorespiratory endurance activity.

If you do not have enough hoops for every child to have one, let them share.

Add an additional signal (e.g., one long whistle) to allow the children to walk and rest.

Safety Tip

Caution the children to watch out for others as they move through general space.

Homework Suggestion

Have children mark a circle on the ground or floor at home using tape, string, or a hoop and practice jumping in and out and running around.

15 Interval Running
Grades: 4-6

Before You Begin

Explain the term *interval training*; teach children how to properly use a stopwatch; discuss what it means to cooperate in a group.

Equipment

Cones; 4 stopwatches.

Organization

Divide the children into four groups. Each group has its own set of cones, stopwatch, and designated area to run. Each group lines up at the end of their running lane (about 40 yards long, made shorter or longer depending on the ability and fitness level of the children).

Procedure

On your signal to begin, each group runs down their lane to the finish line. As they run, one child in the group carries the stopwatch and keeps track of the elapsed time. After everyone in the group has reached the finish line, the stopwatch is stopped and the group rests for a period equal to the running time. After the rest period the children run back the other direction.

Variation

Do this activity without using time as a factor. Instead let children run based on the recovery of their heart rates. This requires that children be able to feel and count the pulse or use heart monitors.

Teaching Tips

Start fourth- to sixth-grade students with five intervals. Adjust the number of intervals to be completed based on fitness levels.

You will have to adjust the running distance to the ability of your children (40 yards is a good starting point for Grades 4-6).

Because one class holds a range of abilities, group the children according to ability so they can stay fairly close together as they run. You can determine their ability levels by monitoring their progress.

Alternate the directions of the runners in adjacent lanes to keep the activity from resembling a relay race.

Remind the children that they are not racing. Each group should work at its own pace.

Let children take turns operating the stopwatches.

Safety Tip

Caution children to watch out for others in their group as they run to the finish line.

Homework Suggestion

Have children practice running intervals at home. (For example, sprint for 20 to 40 yards, walk back to the start, and sprint again.)

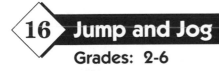

16 Jump and Jog

Grades: 2-6

Before You Begin

Discuss what it means to cooperate with another person; let children practice rope-jumping skills.

Equipment

Music; cones; 1 jump rope for every two children.

Organization

Set up the cones in a large oval or circle (leave enough room on the outside for children to jog). Divide the children into pairs, with each pair getting a jump rope. The child with the rope stands inside the oval; the other child stands outside.

Procedure

The child on the outside of the oval jogs around the cones counterclockwise while the partner jumps rope in place (as shown in Figure 4.5). Give a signal to switch places after 30 to 60 seconds.

Variations

Have children switch roles on their own after the jogger has completed a certain number of laps. (Caution! The oval must be large enough for children to move in and out while others are jumping rope.)

This is a continuous training activity. To adapt it for interval training, group the children in threes. Have one of them rest while the other two exercise, then rotate positions. The resting child can be given a task to work on while waiting (dribbling a ball, tossing and catching a beanbag, etc.).

Teaching Tip

If you are using a cassette tape for music, pauses can be recorded and used as signals for switching roles.

Figure 4.5   In Jump and Jog one partner jumps rope in the center while the other jogs on the outside.

Safety Tips

Caution the joggers not to jog inside the oval. Caution rope jumpers to stay in place inside the oval. Also, they must drop their ropes as soon as you give the signal to switch places.

Homework Suggestion

Have children alternate rope jumping and jogging with a family member.

17 Line Leader

Grades: 2-6

Before You Begin

Discuss what it means to cooperate with a group; let the children practice jogging in a small group, staying close together in a straight line.

Equipment

Cones.

Organization

Divide children into groups of 6 to 8. Each group has its own set of cones, which are set up in an oval or circle, 30 to 50 feet in diameter.

Procedure

On a signal, each group jogs around the circle single-file. The last person in the line runs on the outside of the circle and overtakes the leader. Once in place, the new leader calls "go," and the procedure is repeated. This activity continues, with each person in line becoming the leader.

Variations

Do the procedure in reverse: Have the leader run around the circle until reaching the end of the line. Caution children to jog slowly to avoid fatiguing the runner too much.

Try this activity without circles. Let each group run randomly throughout the area. (This is best done outdoors where the children have more room.)

Teaching Tip

Remind the group to jog (not run) and to stay close together; otherwise the last person will have a difficult time moving into the leader position.

Homework Suggestion

Have children practice playing Line Leader with family members as a fun way to travel throughout the neighborhood.

18 Map Reading and Run
Grades: 2-6

Before You Begin

Review how to interpret a map; discuss what it means to cooperate in a small group; make maps of the area being used (see the appendix for instructions; Figure 4.6 shows a sample map and running course).

Equipment

1 laminated map for every two or three children.

Organization

Divide children into pairs or threes; give each set a map showing a running course.

Procedure

Groups review their maps and determine where they are assigned to run. The children then begin jogging, following the courses outlined. When a group completes the course they may turn in their map for another one and continue.

Variations

Have the children run wherever they want around the designated area for several minutes. Give them drawings of the area and have them draw lines showing where they ran.

Organization

Put baskets, with motion picture cards in them, on the ground in a central location of the running area. The children stand around the baskets.

Procedure

Each child retrieves a motion picture card from a basket. After looking at the photo the child runs to the object pictured, touches it, and returns to the baskets, placing the card face down in one. The child retrieves another card from another basket and repeats the activity.

Variation

To help develop muscular strength and endurance, have an exercise set up at each object, which the child performs upon arriving.

Teaching Tips

After checking the appendix on how to make motion picture cards, keep the following tips in mind:

1. Take photographs of any objects the children would recognize: swingset, monkey bars, trees, play apparatus, benches, steps, doors, markings on the asphalt, rocks, fences, and the like.
2. Make sure that all objects in the photographs can be seen from the basket location.
3. Because the children carry the photographs, it is best to mount them on poster board and laminate them (cut the poster board about a half an inch larger than the picture).

Safety Tip

Caution the children to watch out for other runners because their paths may cross.

Homework Suggestion

Have each child draw pictures of 10 different objects in their backyard or a nearby park or field. The child should place the pictures in a box or bag, pick one at a time, run to the object, then return to the box for another. The activity continues until all pictures have been used.

Movin' to the Beat

Grades: K-3

Before You Begin

Review basic locomotor skills, such as skipping, galloping, and hopping; demonstrate how to slide (a lateral movement, similar to galloping sideways); demonstrate how to "grapevine" (another lateral movement, with the trail foot crossing the lead foot, alternating between front and back); discuss the difference between clockwise and counterclockwise.

Equipment

Tambourine.

Organization

Place children in one large circle, facing the center.

Procedure

To the beat of a tambourine the children perform the following movements in sequence.

Part 1: Slide 16 beats clockwise; slide 16 beats counterclockwise; jog 32 beats clockwise; jog 32 beats counterclockwise.

Part 2: Skip 16 beats clockwise; skip 16 beats counterclockwise; jog 32 beats clockwise; jog 32 beats counterclockwise.

Part 3: Grapevine 16 beats clockwise; grapevine 16 beats counterclockwise; jog 32 beats clockwise; jog 32 beats counterclockwise.

Part 4: Hop 8 beats clockwise; hop 8 beats counterclockwise; jog 32 beats clockwise; jog 32 beats counterclockwise.

Variations

Add new movements to the routine. Perform the routine in a different order. Incorporate Part 4 between the other parts. Develop muscular strength and endurance by performing exercises between each part.

Teaching Tips

With younger children it is best for you to participate in the movement with them.

Teach one part of the routine at a time. Add a new part after children have mastered the previous part.

This is an activity of relatively short duration. You may want to use it as a warm-up or combine it with another cardiorespiratory activity.

Safety Tip

Caution the children to watch where they are going when changing directions.

Homework Suggestion

Have children make up their own routines using four different locomotor movements.

22 ▸ Pennant Fever

Grades: 3-6

Before You Begin

Discuss the term *interval training*; make pennant cards and pennants on wooden stakes (see the appendix for instructions; Figures 4.8 and 4.9 show samples of two different pennant cards); discuss how to interpret the information from the pennant card.

Equipment

Wooden stakes with numbered pennants attached (or cones with numbers on them); pennant fever cards.

Organization

Place stakes in the ground in a circle or oval of about 250-meter (1/4-kilometer) circumference. Each child gets a card and stands at the pennant marked on it.

Procedure

After children have reviewed their cards, give the signal to begin. Using the information on the cards, children run or walk around the outside of the pennant circle.

The card shown in Figure 4.8 uses 10 pennants and shows that the child begins at pennant #6, runs to #8, walks to #10, runs to #2, walks to #4, runs to #5, and walks to #6 to complete 1/4 kilometer.

The card shown in Figure 4.9 uses 8 pennants and represents a pie chart. According to this card, the child begins at pennant #3, runs to #5, walks to #6, runs to #8, walks to #1, runs to #2, and walks to #3 to complete 1/4 kilometer.

Variation

Younger children who cannot interpret the information on the card alternate walking and running from pennant to pennant.

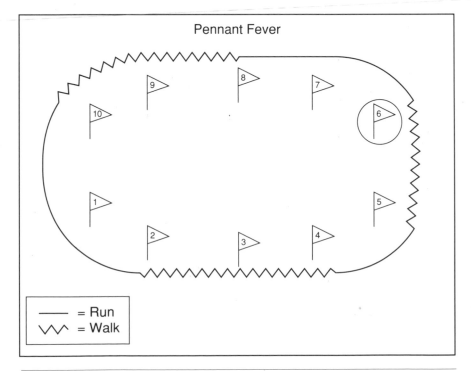

Figure 4.8 A sample interval card for Pennant Fever.

Teaching Tips

Take the time at the beginning of this activity to make sure children understand how to translate the information on the card into movement.

Use this activity to introduce children to different length intervals and different work-to-rest ratios.

A card that exactly resembles the running course (like the one in Figure 4.8) works best for younger children.

Safety Tip

Make a rule that when passing others on the course you must pass on the right.

Homework Suggestion

Have children make up their own pennant cards and bring them to class to use.

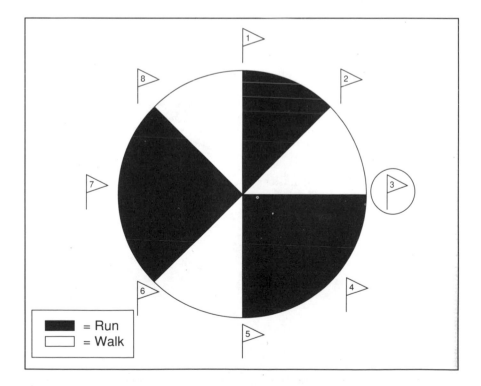

Figure 4.9   A sample interval pie chart for Pennant Fever.

23 ▶ Run-and-Touch Task Card

Grades: 2-6

Before You Begin

Discuss the different objects around your facility (trees, rocks, equipment, fields, parking lots, etc.) and where they are located; make the run-and-touch task cards (see the appendix for instructions; Figure 4.10 shows a sample task card).

Equipment

1 run-and-touch task card for each child; several baskets or boxes.

Organization

Place the baskets, with the task cards inside, on the ground in a central location of the running area. The children stand around the baskets.

Procedure

Each child retrieves a card from one of the baskets. After reading the objects listed, the child runs and touches all of them in order, returns the card to the basket, and retrieves a new one.

Variation

For children who have difficulty reading, try Motion Pictures (Activity #20) instead.

Teaching Tip

List objects that are easy for children to locate and are in full view from the baskets.

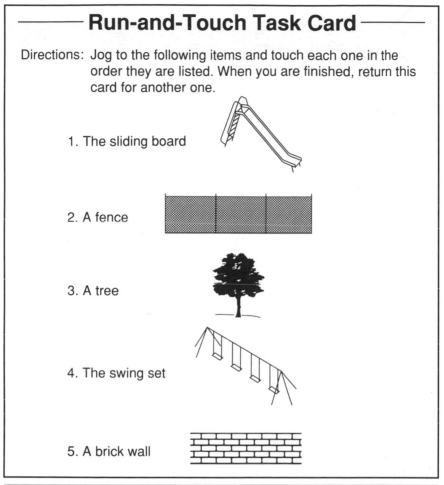

Run-and-Touch Task Card

Directions: Jog to the following items and touch each one in the order they are listed. When you are finished, return this card for another one.

1. The sliding board

2. A fence

3. A tree

4. The swing set

5. A brick wall

Figure 4.10   A sample run-and-touch task card.

Safety Tip

Caution the children to watch out for other runners because their paths may cross.

Homework Suggestion

Have children make up their own run-and-touch task cards and bring them to class.

24 Shuttle Run

Grades: K-6

Before You Begin

Let the children practice stopping, changing direction, and starting again while moving through general space.

Equipment

Cones.

Organization

Divide children into two groups. Both groups stand at one end of the area, divided into four sections with five lines. Each section is 15 to 20 feet wide (see Figure 4.11). Use cones to designate the different areas.

Procedure

As shown in Figure 4.11, Group 1 starts by running from Line 1 to Line 2. After touching Line 2 they return to Line 1, touch it, then run to Line 3. After touching Line 3 they return to Line 2. They then go to Line 4, returning to Line 3. They finish by going to Line 5, returning to Line 4, and finally crossing Line 5. Group 2 runners begin on your signal after Group 1 has reached the halfway point of their run. Once Group 1 runners finish they rest until Group 2 runners finish, then begin again in the opposite direction. This allows the children to work in intervals.

Variation

Each group could run to each of the five lines, always returning to Line 1 before going on. This allows only one group to run at a time, increasing the rest period between intervals, which may decrease the cardio-respiratory benefit of the activity.

Teaching Tips

For younger children start with just one line in the middle. Add other lines after children grasp the idea of the activity. Keep the children moving, allowing only for minimal rest as needed.

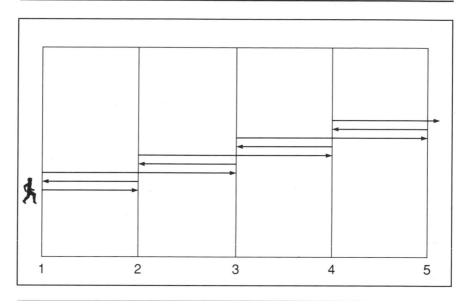

Figure 4.11   A diagram showing the direction the children run from line to line during the Shuttle Run.

Safety Tips

To avoid collisions make sure Group 1 is completely finished touching Line 2 the second time before starting Group 2.

The number of children in each group will determine how wide the area should be. Each child needs 40 to 60 inches of width in which to turn.

Homework Suggestion

Have children practice shuttle running at home by marking off lines in the backyard or on a nearby sidewalk.

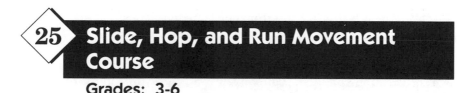

25 Slide, Hop, and Run Movement Course

Grades: 3-6

Before You Begin

Review basic locomotor skills, such as jogging, hopping, and sliding; discuss how to follow a designated course or another person.

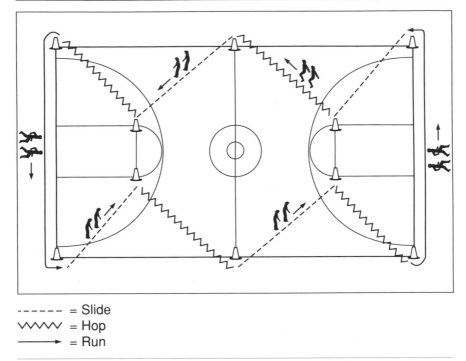

```
------ = Slide
WVWW = Hop
———▶ = Run
```

Figure 4.12   Children moving around the Slide, Hop, and Run course.

Equipment

10 cones.

Organization

Place cones in a zigzag formation as shown in Figure 4.12. Scatter the children throughout the course.

Procedure

The children slide, hop, or run from one cone to the next, working their way around the course. On the ends of the course the children jog (or run). On the sides of the course the children alternate sliding and hopping from cone to cone (see Figure 4.12). On your signal the children reverse direction and work their way around the course in the opposite direction. Continue the activity with numerous directional changes.

Variations

Change the locomotor movements around the course. Establish sections of the course where children can select their own locomotor movements.

Have children manipulate a piece of equipment as they move around the course. Remember, however, if the manipulative skill is difficult it may detract from the cardiorespiratory benefit.

Teaching Tips

Encourage the children to keep moving so the course does not become backed up. Because some children will move faster than others, establish a rule for passing or not passing. Make it clear to children that they are not racing.

Safety Tip

A good rule for passing is to allow it only during the running section of the course.

Homework Suggestion

Have children set up their own slide, hop, and run movement course at home and practice with a family member or friend.

26 Spot Jumping
Grades: K-6

Before You Begin

Review basic locomotor movements, such as skipping, galloping, and jogging; let the children practice moving safely through general space and practice jumping and landing safely.

Equipment

Music; 1 rubber poly spot for each child.

Organization

Scatter the poly spots around the area on the floor. The children are also scattered around the area.

Procedure

When you begin the music the children perform a locomotor movement (you can either designate one or let them choose their own) throughout the area. When you stop the music each child stands on a poly spot. Give the children a jumping task to try. After 10 to 15 seconds of jumping, begin the music again and have children perform a new locomotor movement around the area. The activity continues with the children attempting a different jumping task each time the music stops.

Examples of jumping tasks include the following:

1. Jump on and off the spot.
2. Jump over the spot side to side.
3. Jump over the spot forward and backward.
4. Straddle the spot; jump on and off bringing the feet together.
5. Start with one foot on the spot and one foot off; jump and switch them back and forth.
6. Straddle the spot; jump up touching feet together in the air and landing in a straddle position.

Variations

Use two spots together and perform different jump combinations. Let children create their own ways of jumping on, off, or over the spots.

Teaching Tips

Encourage the children to keep moving. Encourage the children to bend their knees and land on the balls of their feet while jumping.

Safety Tip

Caution the children to watch out for others while moving through general space.

Homework Suggestion

Have children be creative and come up with unique ways to jump on, off, and over the spots. Let them take spots home and practice, then share their discoveries with the rest of the children.

27 Step Aerobics

Grades: 3-6

Before You Begin

Teach the children how to do the basic step-aerobic steps (explained in chapter 3); explain the step safety precautions.

Equipment

Music; (120-125 beats per minute is best; check the appendix for more information on determining beats per minute); 1 aerobic step platform for each child.

Organization

Scatter children around the area standing next to their step platforms.

Procedure

Begin by practicing the following basic steps:

1. Step tap
2. Up/down (right foot lead and left foot lead)
3. Tap step
4. V step
5. Lateral step (across the top)
6. Knee-ups
7. Straddle step
8. Straddle tap step
9. Straddle knee-ups
10. Lunge

As the children master the basic steps, put together a routine. Have the children follow the routine and add to it as they master each step. Keep the children moving during the routine so their heart rates stay elevated. It is best for you to participate in the routine with the children to act as the model for them to copy.

A basic sample routine for novices would go as follows:

- Step tap, 16 counts
- Up/down (right foot lead), 16 counts (last one a tap step)

- Up/down (left foot lead), 16 counts (last one a tap step)
- V step (right foot lead), 16 counts (last one a tap step)
- V step (left foot lead), 16 counts

As the children progress add straddle steps, knee-ups, and lunges. With older children you may want to move to 8 counts of each step.

Variations

Set up several stations around the area with a different step displayed (on a cone card) at each one. Rotate the children around the circuit. If you have only a few step benches, add rope jumping, jogging, or aerobic dance steps (these can be found in chapter 3) to the circuit.

Set up this activity to resemble Jump and Jog (Activity #16). Have one child jog while the other one practices on the step platform.

Teaching Tips

Teach the children how to do several basic steps without using the step platforms.

If you do not have a step platform for each child, put two children at each platform and have one practice the movement on the floor while the other uses the platform. Children then switch places.

Show the children a video of step aerobics or take them on a field trip to a nearby health club to watch a step aerobics class in progress.

Safety Tips

The children need to understand the importance of safety while stepping. Remind them of the following precautions:

1. Make contact with the entire foot when stepping on the platform.
2. Keep eyes on the platform when stepping.
3. Step close to the platform when stepping off.
4. Never step with your back to the platform.

Homework Suggestion

Have children practice the basic steps at home using the bottom step of a set of stairs.

Muscular Strength
and Endurance

The 12 activities in this chapter are designed to help improve muscular strength and endurance in children, along with teaching them important components and principles of fitness. You can adapt most of the activities to an array of ability levels by changing the complexity of the tasks or the intensity and duration at which they are performed. All of the activities require prior knowledge of how to perform certain exercises, which are in chapter 3. Several of the activities require you to make circuit cards or task cards. Information and suggestions on making these cards are in the appendix.

The amount of time you spend on an activity depends largely on children's abilities. I recommend you use these activities for about 8 to 12 minutes, or 25% of your class period. When you first begin muscular strength and endurance activities with young children (specifically grades K-2), small doses are best. I suggest you use light locomotor-type movements or activities, such as jogging or skipping, between short periods focusing on muscular strength and endurance. This breaks up the activity and lets children learn proper execution technique without their muscles becoming too fatigued.

Depending on how much time you have allotted for fitness, you may want to combine one of these activities with a cardiorespiratory endurance activity from chapter 4 or a flexibility activity from chapter 6. This gives a more balanced workout and offers some variety in your lesson.

Remember to explain and utilize key components and principles of fitness before, during, and after the activities to broaden children's fitness knowledge via hands-on experience.

1 Ball Exercises

Grades: K-6

Before You Begin

Discuss *weight (resistance) training*. Explain its purpose in strengthening muscles and the importance of proper form.

Equipment

Music; 2 balls (or similar objects weighing 5-16 ounces) for each child (e.g., tennis balls, beanbags).

Organization

Scatter children around the area; they hold one ball in each hand.

Procedure

With music playing, lead the children through 10 to 20 repetitions of the following exercises (see chapter 3 to find out how to perform them):

1. Bent-over rowing
2. Biceps curl
3. Lateral deltoid lift
4. Overhead press
5. Overhead triceps extension
6. Shoulder shrug
7. Single-arm rowing
8. Upright rowing

Variation

Combine this activity with a cardiorespiratory workout by having children jog around the area between exercises.

Teaching Tips

This activity is to teach proper form and technique when performing basic resistance-training exercises. The weight of the balls should be very light. They are used less for the resistance than as props to give children the feel for doing the exercise. The order of the exercises is not important.

Use this activity as a lead-up to weight training or resistance training (see Resistance-Training Circuit, Activity #12).

After the children have developed proper form, let them experiment with objects of different sizes and weights in their hands while performing the exercises.

Safety Tip

Remind the children to perform the movements in a slow and controlled manner. Caution them on proper form and body alignment.

Homework Suggestion

Have students practice the ball exercises at home using tennis balls or other small balls.

2 Beat the Bell

Grades: K-3

Before You Begin

Teach the children basic muscular strength and endurance exercises (suggested exercises are in chapter 3); let them practice moving safely through general space.

Equipment

Music; 1 poly spot for each child; 2 Indian clubs (or plastic bowling pins); 1 bell.

Organization

Scatter children around the area, each standing on a poly spot. The Indian clubs are laid next to the bell in the center of the area.

Procedure

Before beginning, choose an exercise, such as push-ups, to be used for the first turn. When you begin the music, the children perform a loco-motor movement around the area (you can choose it or let them do so). When you stop the music all children quickly move to poly spots and begin doing the designated exercise. At the same time, call one child's name. The child who is called goes to the center, stands up the two Indian clubs, and rings the bell. The object is to see how many exercise repetitions can be completed before the bell is rung. Each child infor-mally keeps track of her or his repetitions. When the bell rings, a new exercise is chosen for the second turn. When you begin the music again, the children continue their movement around the area.

Variation

You can make Beat the Bell a vigorous cardiorespiratory activity by using aerobic dance exercises instead of muscular strength and endur-ance exercises (you can find a description of aerobic dance exercises in chapter 3).

Teaching Tips

If you don't know children's names, assign numbers and use them to identify who goes to the center.

Speed is not the focus of this activity. Discourage children from per-forming exercises of poor quality to gain quantity. Do not focus on num-bers of repetitions; it is not a contest to see who can do the most. In-stead it is an individual and personal challenge.

If you want children to perform more repetitions of each exercise, simply add more Indian clubs at the center.

Safety Tip

Caution the children to watch out for others as they move through general space, especially when they hurry to find a poly spot.

Homework Suggestion

Have children practice the exercises they learn in class at home so they can become more efficient at performing them.

3 ▷ Circuit Training

Grades: 2-6

Before You Begin

Make 12 circuit training cards (see the appendix for instructions; Figure 5.1 shows a sample 12-station circuit); make sure the children can read the information on the circuit cards; explain the term *circuit training*.

Equipment

Music; 12 circuit training cards; 12 cones.

Organization

Place the cones, with the cards on them, in an oval or circle around the perimeter of the area. Place two or three children at each cone.

Procedure

When you begin the music the children perform the exercise written on the card at their station. On a signal (a break in the music or a whistle), all children move one station counterclockwise and begin the next exercise immediately. The activity continues until all children have completed each station.

Variations

For younger children, write the name of an animal on the circuit card. When switching stations the children must move like that animal. (This is shown on the cards in Figure 5.1.) You can also write locomotor movements on the cards. For younger children who have difficulty reading, paste pictures of the animals next to the names.

Instead of having children move in a circle, number the stations randomly and have them do a movement around the area until they locate the next number in sequence.

Let the children choose where they want to go next. It may seem chaotic at first, but as long as you limit how many children can be at a station at a time it will work out fine.

Figure 5.1 A sample 12-station circuit to build muscular strength and endurance.

Teaching Tips

Although the children are in groups, encourage them to exercise at their own pace. To help children who have difficulty reading, place higher level readers at stations with lower level readers.

Safety Tip

Remind the children to allow ample room between themselves and others in their group when performing the exercises.

Homework Suggestion

Have children design their own five-station circuit to be used at home with friends and family members.

 **Color-Coded Exercises**

Grades: 3-6

Before You Begin

Make color-coded exercise cards (see the appendix for instructions; Figure 5.2 shows samples); make sure the children can read the cards; let the children practice moving safely through general space.

Equipment

Music; color-coded exercise cards; 1 hoop for each child (in 4 different colors to match the cards).

Organization

Scatter the hoops on the floor around the area. Each child stands inside a hoop; you stand holding the cards, in full view of all children.

Procedure

When you begin the music, the children perform a locomotor movement around the area (you can choose it or let them do so) without touching the hoops. When you stop the music, each child stops inside a hoop and you hold up the first card, which has four exercises listed and

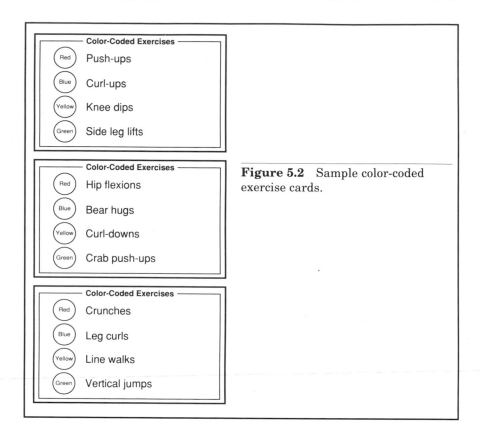

Figure 5.2 Sample color-coded exercise cards.

labeled with colors. The children perform the exercise that matches the color of the hoop they are in. After 15 to 30 seconds begin the music again; the children begin moving around the area. The activity continues, with you holding up a new card on each turn.

Variation

Instead of colored hoops use poly spots and write the colors on the spots with a colored marker. Children will have to read the words to do the correct exercise. Or instead of writing the colors you can use colored poly spots, draw shapes on the poly spots, or use shape-coded cards.

Teaching Tips

Make the cards at least 8-1/2 by 11 inches—the larger they are, the easier it is for the children to see the exercise. Stand in a central location and rotate as you hold up the card, or stand off on the perimeter. You can help nonreaders by calling out the colors and their exercises.

Safety Tip

Caution the children to watch out for others while moving through general space.

Homework Suggestion

Have children make a color-coded exercise card with four of their favorite exercises on it and bring it to the next physical education class.

5 ▶ Exercise Task Cards

Grades: 2-6

Before You Begin

Make the task cards (see the appendix for instructions; Figure 5.3 shows a sample); make sure children can read the cards; teach children the exercises you have included on the cards (suggested exercises are in chapter 3); explain the terms *sets* and *repetitions*.

Equipment

Music; 1 task card for each child; miscellaneous resistance training equipment (2- to 4-lb. dumbbells, chairs, rubber tubing).

Exercise Task Card

> Directions: Perform 2 sets of each of the following exercises. Return this card for another one when you are finished.

1. 10 biceps curls (Use either 2-lb. dumbbells or rubber tubing.)
2. 8 wall squats
3. 6 chair dips
4. 10 crunches
5. 5 side leg lifts with each leg

Figure 5.3 A sample exercise task card.

Organization

The children, scattered around the area, each receive a task card. Scatter the equipment around the area for the children to use.

Procedure

When you begin the music, children perform in order the exercises written on their cards. After completing all the activities listed, children return their cards for another.

Variation

This activity can be done in groups of two to four children, with the group sharing a card. This helps children who have difficulty reading.

Teaching Tips

Set up different areas or stations where certain exercises should be performed. Let the children perform the exercises in any order, at their own pace. Use this activity to teach about sets and repetitions.

Safety Tips

Caution the children to watch out for others as they do their exercises and move around the area. Remind children of proper form and execution of each exercise.

Homework Suggestion

Have children make an exercise task card to be used at home and the next time they come to class.

6 ▸ Fitness Bag

Grades: 2-6

Before You Begin

Make fitness bags and puzzles (see the appendix for instructions; Figure 5.4 shows sample puzzles); discuss with the children what it means to cooperate in a group; make sure they can read the puzzle pieces; teach the exercises you include in your puzzles (suggested exercises are in chapter 3).

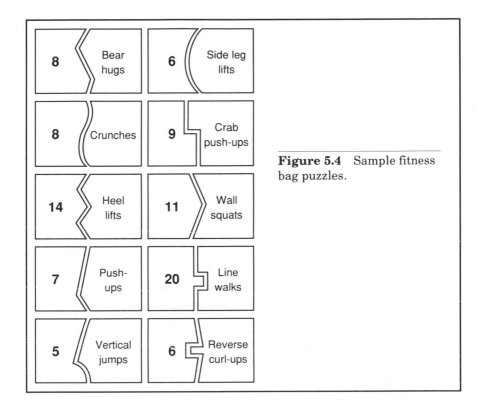

Figure 5.4   Sample fitness bag puzzles.

Equipment

1 fitness bag for every 2 or 3 children.

Organization

Place children in groups of two or three. Each group receives a fitness bag.

Procedure

The group opens the bag and spreads the puzzle pieces out on the floor. Working together, the group matches all the pieces. After all pieces are matched the children perform each exercise written on the puzzle cards. When they complete an exercise they return the puzzle pieces to the bag and perform the next exercise. The activity continues until all the pieces have been returned to the bag.

Teaching Tips

It is best to do this activity indoors because the puzzle pieces can be easily blown away.

Make sure there are enough puzzles in the bag that children can work for the 8- to 12-minute period (10-15 puzzles per bag). Otherwise some groups will finish before others.

Safety Tips

Caution the children to watch out for others as they move throughout the area.

If you use locomotor movements in this activity, the children should perform the exercises away from where other children are moving around.

Homework Suggestion

Have children make their own puzzles to use at home and to bring to the next physical education class.

7 Fitnopoly

Grades: K-6

Before You Begin

Make the Fitnopoly boards (see the appendix for instructions; Figure 5.5 shows a sample); discuss what it means to cooperate in a small group; if the children are going to play on their own, make sure they can read the board; teach them the exercises you have included (suggested exercises are in chapter 3).

Equipment

1 Fitnopoly game board for every 3 or 4 children; 1 die for each game board; 1 game piece (any small object will do, such as a stone, coin, or toy) for each child.

Organization

Place children in groups of three or four. Each group receives a game board and a die. Each child has a game piece. The group selects a place around the perimeter of the area in which to play.

Figure 5.5 A sample Fitnopoly game board.

Procedure

The object of the game is for each player to take a turn rolling the die and moving the game piece along the board toward the finish line. After each roll the player moves the game piece the number of spaces shown on the die and performs the exercise or activity that the game piece lands on. While Player A is performing, Player B rolls the die and takes a turn. Player C follows, and so on. The game continues until one player reaches the finish line on the board.

Variations

Each group can play with one game piece, with all members of the group performing the same task on each roll.

With nonreaders you can play the game in a large group with you reading the tasks and the entire group doing the activity together (this is the best way to play with grades K-2).

Teaching Tips

It is fun to use large foam dice (available from various equipment suppliers).

The Fitnopoly boards should be made on poster board (about 18 by 24 inches) for sturdiness.

You will probably want to make boards with different activities and exercises to meet a range of abilities. (A board that first graders use will have to be different from one sixth graders use.)

Safety Tip

If the tasks on the game board involve moving through general space, remind the children to watch out for others as they move.

Homework Suggestion

Have children make their own Fitnopoly boards on standard sheets of paper to play at home with their family and friends. Have them bring the boards to class to use or to share.

Group Secret Exercises

Grades: K-3

Before You Begin

Make the secret exercise cards (see the appendix for instructions; Figure 5.6 shows samples); let the children practice moving safely through general space; teach them the exercises you have included on the cards (suggested exercises are in chapter 3).

Equipment

Music; 10 to 15 secret exercise cards.

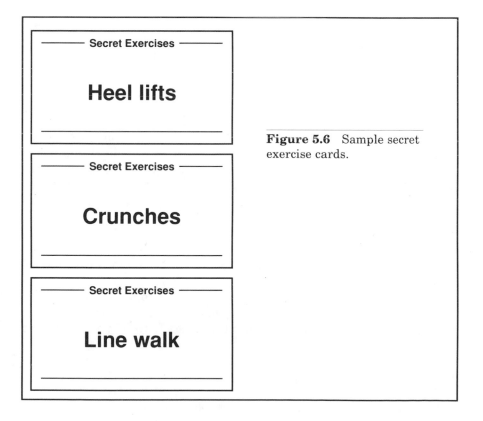

——— Secret Exercises ———

Heel lifts

——— Secret Exercises ———

Crunches

——— Secret Exercises ———

Line walk

Figure 5.6 Sample secret exercise cards.

Organization

Place the cards face down in the center of the area. Scatter children around the area.

Procedure

When you begin the music, the children perform a locomotor movement around the area (you can choose it or let them do so). When you stop the music, the children stop and one child is selected to turn over a card in the center. The exercise on the card is read aloud and the children all perform the exercise. When you begin the music again, the children move around the area using a different locomotor movement. The activity continues, with a different child chosen each time to turn over a card.

Variations

This activity can be performed without the locomotor movements. Have the child who turns over the card perform the exercise while the other children try to guess its name. After it is guessed all the children perform it. This helps the children learn the names of the exercises.

Teaching Tips

Use this activity to teach children how to execute specific exercises. This activity can offer cardiorespiratory benefits if the children are kept moving and cards are turned over quickly. If the children do not read well enough, you can help them read the cards. This activity does not work well outdoors on windy days.

Safety Tips

Caution the children to watch out for others while moving throughout the area.

The children tend to congregate in the center to see the card being turned over. Remind them to move away from others before performing the exercises so that they do not hit others with moving arms and legs.

Homework Suggestion

Have children make their own secret exercise cards to use at home with friends and family. Have them bring their cards to class to use.

Individual Secret Exercises

Grades: 3-6

Before You Begin

Make the secret exercise cards (see the appendix for instructions; Figure 5.6 shows samples); let the children practice moving safely through general space; make sure the children can read and perform the exercises you have included (suggested exercises are in chapter 3).

Equipment

Music; 1 secret exercise card and 1 poly spot for each child.

Organization

Scatter the poly spots around the area with an exercise card placed face up under each one. Scatter the children around the area, with each standing on a poly spot.

Procedure

When you begin the music, the children perform a locomotor movement around the area (you can choose it or let them do so) without touching the poly spots. When you stop the music, each child quickly goes to a poly spot, lifts it up, reads the exercise written on the card, then places the spot back over the card. The child performs that exercise. When the music begins children move around the area again. The activity continues, with the children stopping at a new spot whenever the music is stopped.

Variations

Divide the area into sections, such as upper body, lower body, legs, arms, and shoulders. Place the appropriate exercise cards in that section. Require the children to perform exercises in every section.

Instead of using cards with muscular strength and endurance exercises on them, use cards with flexibility or cardiorespiratory exercises.

Add a locomotor movement to the card. When children finish the exercise they move around the area according to the movement on the card.

Teaching Tips

Make a rule that you cannot stop at the same poly spot more than once. Set out more poly spots and cards than there are children to help decrease the time it takes to find a vacant spot.

To help children who have difficulty reading, pair higher level readers with lower level readers. Let the children share spots (placing two or three children together works fine).

Play the music about 15 to 20 seconds at a time and allow the children 15 to 20 seconds to perform an exercise.

Safety Tip

Caution the children to watch out for others while moving through general space.

Homework Suggestion

Have children make their own set of individual secret exercise cards and play at home with their friends and family members. Have them bring their cards to the next physical education class.

10 ▸ Parachute Exercises
Grades: K-3

Before You Begin

Teach the children how to perform the exercises to be used (see chapter 3).

Equipment

Music; 1 parachute (about 24 feet in diameter); assorted lightweight balls.

Organization

Spread out the parachute on the floor. Children sit evenly spaced around the perimeter of the parachute. Place the balls on the parachute when needed.

Procedure

Children perform 10 to 20 repetitions of the following exercises as the music is played:

1. Seated facing the parachute—biceps curl, rowing, and front deltoid lift
2. Seated with back to the parachute—overhead triceps extension
3. Standing facing the parachute—biceps curl, upright rowing, and front deltoid lift
4. Standing with back to the parachute—overhead triceps extension
5. Standing with right side to the parachute—lateral deltoid lift (right arm)
6. Standing with left side to the parachute—lateral deltoid lift (left arm)

The balls will roll around and jump up and down with the movement of the parachute. This makes the activity more exciting for young children.

Variation

With each child holding on to the parachute with one hand, jog around in a circle between exercises.

Teaching Tip

Work on getting all the children to execute the movement at the same time. This increases the amount of resistance everyone feels because the parachute will be pulled in all directions at once.

Safety Tip

Remind the children not to jerk on the parachute. Instead they should perform smooth movements.

Homework Suggestion

Assign exercises for children to practice at home with another family member using a towel, bed sheet, or blanket.

11 ⟩ Partner Circuit Training

Grades: 2-6

Before You Begin

Make the partner circuit cards (see the appendix for instructions; Figure 5.7 shows samples); make sure the children can read and perform the exercises you include (suggested exercises are in chapter 3).

Equipment

Music; cones; partner circuit cards.

Organization

Place the cones, with the circuit cards on them, in a circle or oval around the perimeter of the area, forming a 12-station circuit. Assign the children to pairs.

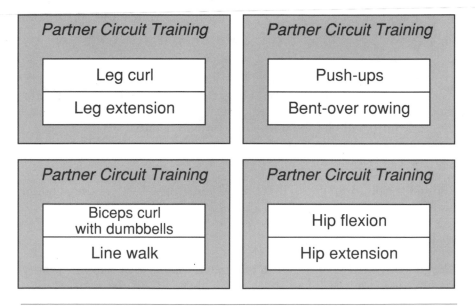

Figure 5.7   Sample partner circuit training cards.

Procedure

When you begin the music, one child in the group performs the exercise written on the top half of the card. The other child performs the exercise written on the bottom half. At a signal (a break in the music or a whistle), the children switch exercises. After both children have completed both parts, the pair moves on to the next station. This procedure continues until the children have completed the circuit.

Variations

Let both children do the same exercise together at each station for a specified time or number of repetitions.

Write an animal name or paste a picture of an animal (or both) on each station card. The children must imitate that animal as they move to the next station (for an example refer back to Figure 5.1, in Activity #3).

Add a cardiorespiratory workout to this activity by making one of the exercises a locomotor movement around the area or an aerobic dance exercise.

Place the children in threes. Have one child jog while the other two perform the exercises. The children rotate places on the signal.

Teaching Tips

Let children choose the order in which they do the stations. This facilitates decision making and cooperation.

Several of the stations can require one child to help the other perform the exercise.

Safety Tip

If you add locomotor movements remind the children to all move in the same direction.

Homework Suggestion

Have children create their own circuit and practice it at home with another family member as a partner.

Resistance-Training Circuit

Grades: 3-6

Before You Begin

Make the weight training picture cards (see the appendix for instructions); teach the children how to do the exercises you include (suggested exercises are in chapter 3); discuss the importance of proper execution and form for each exercise.

Equipment

1 set of dumbbells for each child (about 1-4 lb each or a weight suitable for the children's ability); cones; weight training picture cards.

Organization

Place the cones, with the training cards on them, in a large circle or oval around the perimeter of the area. Place the children in groups of three or four, each group standing at a different station with dumbbells at each one. Depending on the ability of the children, upper body exercise stations should have 1- to 3-lb dumbbells, and lower body exercise stations should have 2- to 4-lb dumbbells.

Procedure

On a signal to begin, the children perform the exercise shown on the training card at their station. After about 30 seconds give the signal to move to the next station. The children rotate counterclockwise to the next station and begin the next exercise. This procedure continues until the circuit is completed.

Exercises you might put on the picture cards include these (shown in chapter 3):

- Bent-over rowing
- Biceps curl
- Lateral deltoid lift
- Overhead press
- Overhead triceps extension
- Shoulder shrug
- Single-arm rowing
- Upright rowing

Variation

Set up aerobic dance exercise stations between weight training stations.

Teaching Tips

Spend some time working on lifting technique without using the dumbbells. Use Ball Exercises (Activity #1) as a lead-up to this activity.

Some children may find 1- to 4-lb dumbbells to be too light. Remind them that at a young age learning proper form and technique is more important than lifting heavy weights.

Music can be used in this activity, but you may want to begin without it. This lets you offer verbal tips on proper exercise execution without the children being distracted.

Safety Tip

Caution the children on proper execution when using weights.

Homework Suggestion

Send home a handout showing the exercises; have children practice the weight training exercises without weights so they can improve their technique.

Flexibility

The eight activities in this chapter are designed to improve flexibility in children while they learn its importance. All of the activities use the same 22 stretching exercises (14 static stretches and 8 dynamic stretches) that are in chapter 3. Choose the exercises that meet your needs according to the children's ability and your objectives. Because many young children have a difficult time understanding the concept of holding a muscle in a stretched position, it is often best to begin with dynamic stretches.

Spend time at the beginning teaching the children proper stretching technique. Explain what a stretched muscle should and should not feel like, and give the children opportunities to explore this feeling. After this is accomplished you can begin teaching them how to stretch various muscles.

After the children have learned the stretching exercises and have had experience with these activities, you may want to use them as a warm-up and cool-down for the activities in chapters 4 and 5. This helps prepare children for vigorous exercise and helps to reduce muscle soreness.

In several of the activities I suggest you use music. If you do, slow, relaxing music is best. Upbeat music contradicts the mood you want to set for stretching.

As I mentioned in chapters 4 and 5, use each activity as an opportunity to teach the children about an important fitness component or principle. When they can use—in a hands-on manner—the information you share, they are better able to learn it.

 ## Flexibility Circuit
Grades: 3-6

Before You Begin

Make the flexibility circuit cards (see the appendix for instructions; Figure 6.1 shows samples); teach the children how to do the flexibility exercises you include (suggested exercises are in chapter 3).

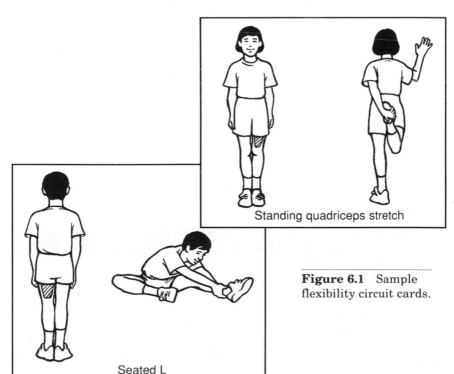

Standing quadriceps stretch

Seated L

Figure 6.1 Sample flexibility circuit cards.

Equipment

Music (slow, relaxing); 12 cones; 12 flexibility circuit cards.

Organization

Set up the cones, with the cards on them, in a large circle or oval around the perimeter of the area. Divide the children into groups of two or three; each group stands at a different station.

Procedure

When the music begins the children perform the stretches displayed on their cards. After 15 to 30 seconds give the signal to relax. After a short relaxation period (5 to 10 seconds), have children repeat the same stretch on the opposite side of the body. On the next signal they rotate counterclockwise to the next station.

Teaching Tip

Because this activity relies on children's stretching on their own, it is important to circulate around the area and offer corrective feedback. The more time you spend teaching the children proper stretching technique, the better they will be at stretching on their own.

Safety Tip

Remind the children to stretch in a slow and controlled manner for static stretches. Caution them about bouncing as they stretch.

Homework Suggestion

Assign three to six of the stretches learned to be practiced at home.

2 Flexibility Photo

Grades: 2-6

Before You Begin

Make the flexibility photo cards (see the appendix for instructions); teach the children the exercises you include (suggested exercises are in chapter 3).

Equipment

Flexibility photo cards; baskets or boxes.

Organization

Place flexibility photo cards in the baskets in the center of the area. Divide the children into two groups. Give each child in Group 1 a photo card. Group 2 has no photo cards to start.

Procedure

The children in Group 1 begin by performing the stretching exercises shown on their photo cards. They hold the stretch for 15 seconds, relax for 5 seconds, then repeat the stretch for 15 more seconds (I usually let children keep track of their own time). When finished they return their cards to the baskets, jog one lap, then retrieve more cards. Group 2 follows the same procedure, but they begin by jogging one lap first. (This helps to alleviate crowds at the baskets at the start.) Note: The children should stretch both right and left sides of the body even though the photograph may only show one side.

Variations

This activity can be done in pairs—one child jogs while the other stretches, then they switch places.

Label the baskets for different body parts and have the children select from a different basket each time.

Teaching Tips

Because this activity relies on the children stretching on their own, it is important to circulate around the area and offer corrective feedback. The more time you spend on teaching the children proper stretching technique, the better they will be at stretching on their own.

Designate an area for jogging and an area for stretching.

Safety Tips

Make sure the children know which area of the site is used for jogging and which is used for stretching. (You don't want joggers stepping on stretchers!)

Caution the children not to bounce as they stretch for static stretches. Remind them to move in a slow and controlled manner.

Homework Suggestion

Assign three to six of the stretches learned to be practiced at home.

3 ▸ Flexibility Tag

Grades: K-4

Before You Begin

Make the flexibility tag cards (see the appendix for instructions; Figure 6.2 shows sample cards); let the children practice moving safely through general space; teach the exercises you include on the cards (suggested exercises are in chapter 3); make sure the children can read

---

Flexibility Tag
_____

Butterfly

Figure 6.2   Sample flexibility tag cards.

Flexibility Tag
_____

Knee to chest

Flexibility Tag
_____

Body circle

the exercises on their cards and know how to do them based on the name (remember, there are no pictures).

Equipment

Music; flexibility tag cards.

Organization

Scatter the children throughout the area, half with flexibility tag cards.

Procedure

When the music begins the children with the tag cards attempt to tag someone without a card. When tagged, the child takes the tag card from the tagger and performs the stretching exercise written on it for 15 seconds. The exercisers then become taggers and try to tag someone who does not have a card.

Variation

You can do this activity without flexibility tag cards by designating a particular stretching exercise to be performed. (This is the best way to play with Grades K-1.) Select several children to be taggers. Someone who is tagged must perform the designated exercise for 15 seconds (I usually let the children do their own counting), then try to tag someone else. Switch the designated exercise throughout the game in order to stretch different body parts.

Teaching Tips

If children receive the same card more than once, they repeat the stretching exercise.

You may have to adjust the ratio of children with cards to those without depending on the size of the group.

Safety Tips

Caution the children to watch out for others as they move through general space. Remind the children who are stretching to do so around the perimeter of the area so runners don't collide with them.

Caution the children not to bounce as they stretch for static stretches. Remind them to move in a slow and controlled manner.

Homework Suggestion

Have children make their own flexibility tag cards and play with friends or family members at home. Or have them teach their parents how to perform the stretching exercises they've learned. Have them bring their cards to class.

4 **Flexibility Task Card**
Grades: 3-6

Before You Begin

Make the flexibility task cards (see the appendix for instructions; Figure 6.3 shows a sample); teach the children how to do the exercises you include (suggested exercises are in chapter 3); make sure the children can read the cards.

F l e x i b i l i t y

Directions: After warming up your muscles, perform the
following stretches for 15 seconds each.
Remember to do both right and left sides.

1. Seated-L
2. Standing quadriceps
3. Butterfly
4. Shoulder rolls
5. Overhead reach

T a s k C a r d

Figure 6.3 A sample flexibility task card.

Equipment

1 task card for each child.

Organization

Scatter the children around the area.

Procedure

Give each child a task card and have children perform the stretches in the order listed on their cards. After completing all stretches each child returns the card to you. If time permits, give out second cards and let children continue.

Variation

Let the children perform locomotor movements between stretches.

Teaching Tips

If some children need help reading, this activity can be done in pairs or small groups.

To help children who are not sure how to perform all stretches, hang pictures of the stretches on the wall around the area. Remind the children to take their time and perform all stretches correctly.

Safety Tip

Caution children not to bounce as they stretch. They should always stretch in a slow and controlled manner.

Homework Suggestion

Have children make their own flexibility task cards and practice stretching at home. Have them bring the cards to their next physical education class.

Figure 6.4   Sample magic box flexibility cards.

5 ▶ Magic Box
Grades: 2-6

Before You Begin

Make a magic box and the exercise cards to go in it (see the appendix for instructions; Figure 6.4 shows sample cards); teach the children how to do the exercises you include (suggested exercises are in chapter 3); make sure the children can read the cards.

Equipment

Music (slow, relaxing); 1 magic box; assorted magic box flexibility cards.

Organization

Place the box in the center of the area with the cards inside. Scatter the children around the area. Give half of the children their own cards (when using this activity as a warm-up, hand cards out as children enter the area).

Procedure

When you begin the music the children with cards perform the stretching exercises displayed on their cards. The other children go to the magic box and retrieve a card. (This divides the children to avoid a crowd at the box.) After retrieving cards they too perform the exercises shown. As children complete their exercises they return their cards to the box and take another. Continue until the allotted time has elapsed.

Variations

Have children work in pairs or small groups to decrease the number of children who have to go to the box.

Use more than one box. Label each box for different body parts. Require the children to visit every box.

Have the children exchange cards with a classmate instead of going back to the box for a new card.

You can do this activity with Grades K-1 by letting one child pull out a card and having the entire group follow you as you perform the stretch.

Teaching Tips

Help children who do not understand their stretches. Remind the children not to rush through their stretching exercises. A few children may view this activity as a race to see who can complete the most cards.

Safety Tips

Caution the children to move with care as they approach and depart from the box. It can become a crowded area. Remind children to stretch in a slow and controlled manner.

Homework Suggestion

Have children make their own flexibility cards and put them in a shoe box to play Magic Box at home with friends or family members. Have them bring the box to class for everyone to use.

6   Muscle Match

Grades: 4-6

Before You Begin

Make the muscle match cards (see the appendix for instructions; Figure 6.5 shows a sample); teach children the exercises, what body parts to stretch, and the appropriate names (suggested exercises are in chapter 3).

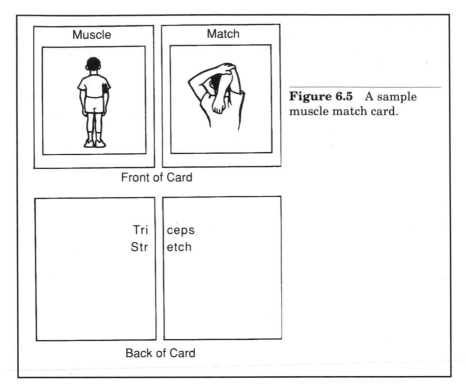

Figure 6.5 A sample muscle match card.

Equipment

Music (slow, relaxing); 1 set of muscle match cards for every two or three children (a set consists of all the exercises you want the children to perform).

Organization

Place the children in groups of two or three. Each group receives a set of muscle match cards.

Procedure

The children spread the cards on the floor with the pictures facing up. Each group then works together to match the pictures showing the muscles with the pictures showing the corresponding stretches. After all cards have been matched the children turn the cards over to check their answers, then perform the stretches shown on the cards for 15 seconds. The group is finished when they have completed all of the exercises.

Teaching Tips

Most groups will not finish at the same time. When a group finishes before the others, ask them to repeat several stretches, or have another activity for them to begin.

Flexibility Circuit (Activity #1) is a good lead-up to this activity because it helps children recognize which exercises are used to stretch certain muscles.

This activity is very helpful in assessing what children have learned about body parts, muscles, and stretching.

Safety Tip

Caution the children not to bounce as they stretch for static stretches. Remind them to stretch in a slow and controlled manner.

Homework Suggestion

Have children practice at home the stretches they learned in class.

7 Secret Stretches
Grades: 3-6

Before You Begin

Make the Secret Stretch cards (see the appendix for instructions; to avoid having to make additional cards, use the ones from Activity #5, Magic Box, or from Activity #3, Flexibility Tag); teach the children how to do the exercises you include; discuss how to cooperate with a group; let the children practice moving in small groups through general space.

Equipment

Music (slow, relaxing); flexibility cards; baskets.

Organization

Place the children in groups of four. Each group forms a single-file line. Place the flexibility cards in the baskets in the center of the area.

Procedure

When you begin the music each group jogs around the area, staying together in a line. When you stop the music the leader of each group (the person at front of the line) runs to the center, picks up a flexibility card, returns to the group, and leads them in the stretching exercise shown on the card. When the music begins again the group resumes jogging. The leader returns the card to the basket and rejoins the group at the end of the line. The new line leader retrieves the next card when the music is stopped again. The activity continues with each group member receiving a chance to be the group leader.

Variations

Do the activity in pairs instead of in groups of four.

Scatter stations around the area, each with a different stretching exercise displayed. When the music stops the group leader stops at the nearest station and the group performs that exercise. Have at least one station per group and start the activity with each group at a different station. Make a rule that the group must go to a different station each time.

Teaching Tips

Give groups ample time to perform their stretches before beginning the music again. Usually it takes about 30 to 40 seconds.

Remind the groups to jog at a slow to moderate pace. This allows the child who is returning the card to catch up to the end of the line.

Safety Tips

Caution the children to watch out for other groups as they move through general space. Caution the children not to bounce as they stretch.

Homework Suggestion

Have children practice at home the stretches they learned in class.

8 ▶ Stretch-N-Go

Grades: K-6

Before You Begin

Make the stretching poster (see the appendix for instructions; Figure 6.6 shows a sample); teach the children the exercises on the poster; let the children practice moving safely through general space.

Equipment

Music or tambourine; poster listing the stretching exercises to be performed.

Organization

Scatter the children around the area. Display the poster so everyone can see it.

Procedure

When you begin the music (or start beating the tambourine), the children perform a locomotor movement around the area. When you stop the music the children stop moving; select one child to choose a stretching exercise from the poster. The child leads the class in that stretch (with younger children it is usually necessary for you to lead). The activity continues with a new locomotor movement and another leader.

Variation

Each time the music stops have children choose their own stretch to perform; they must choose a different one each time.

Teaching Tips

Instead of making a poster, you can write the names of the exercises on a chalk board. To avoid focusing on children who may not wish to lead, ask for volunteer leaders.

Figure 6.6   A sample wall poster for static flexibility exercise.

Safety Tips

Caution the children to watch out for others as they move through general space.

Caution the children not to bounce for static stretches. Remind them to stretch in a slow and controlled manner.

Homework Suggestion

Have children make up a list of their favorite stretches and practice them at home. Have them bring their lists to class and use them to pick from.

Appendix

Making the Equipment You Need

Making Circuit Cards for Cones

This section explains how to make cards for these five activities:

- Aerobic Dance Circuit
- Cardio Circuit
- Circuit Training
- Partner Circuit Training
- Flexibility Circuit

Materials

Manila file folders (available at office supply stores for $3-$4 per 100), colored markers, scissors, stapler, and laminating machine.

Procedure

1. With the folder closed, trim off and discard the tabs as shown in Figure A.1 (folders without tabs are also available).

2. Leave the folder closed and cut a 1-inch strip the length of the folder (see Figure A.2). Save these strips.

3. Open the folder and cut it in half at the fold (see Figure A.3). You now have two cards and two backing strips.

4. Write, draw, or paste your pictures or directions (or both) on the cards. Add any decorations you wish. (Samples of many of these cards can be found in chapters 4, 5, and 6.)

5. Laminate the cards and the strips.

6. Staple each strip to the back of a card (see Figure A.4).

7. Open the strip and suspend the card on a cone (see Figure A.5).

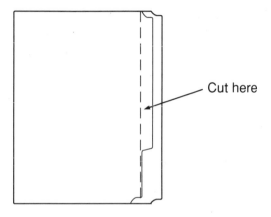

Cut here

Figure A.1   Trim off the tabs along the edges.

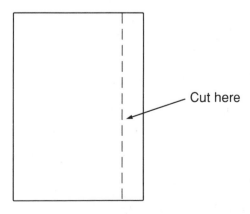

Cut here

Figure A.2   Cut 1-inch strips.

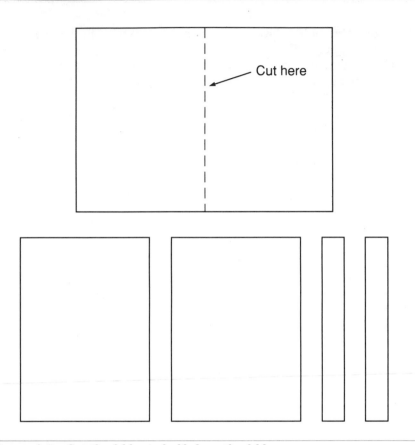

Figure A.3   Cut the folder in half along the fold.

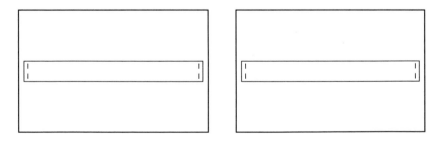

Figure A.4   Staple the strips to the backs of the cards.

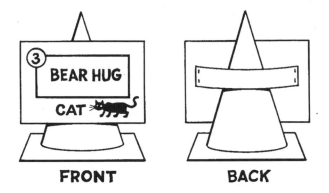

FRONT   **BACK**

Figure A.5   Place the card over a cone.

Making Cards With Photographs

This section explains how to make cards for these activities:

- Motion Pictures
- Resistance-Training Circuit
- Flexibility Photo

Motion Pictures

Take photographs of objects around your facility that children will recognize (doors, trees, swingsets, fences, monkey bars, play apparatus, pavement markings, benches, slides, etc.).

Have double prints made of the photographs when you get the film developed (there is usually a nominal fee). This will give you twice as many cards for children to use.

To mount the photographs on cards, follow the directions just given for making circuit cards, skipping Step 2. (You will not need the backing strips because these cards do not get placed on cones.)

Resistance-Training Circuit

Photograph a child in the starting position of a resistance exercise from chapter 3. This will be the beginning of the concentric phase of the contraction. Have the child perform one repetition, and take another picture when the child reaches the end of the concentric phase, just before the eccentric phase begins. Repeat this procedure for each resistance exercise you want the children to do.

After the film is developed, follow the directions on pages 144-146 to mount the photographs on cards for use on cones.

Make sure you mount both photos of each exercise on the same card (as shown in Figure A.6). This shows the children the starting position and where to move next.

Flexibility Photo

Photograph a child in the correct stretching position for a flexibility exercise from chapter 3. Repeat this procedure for each flexibility exercise you want the children to do.

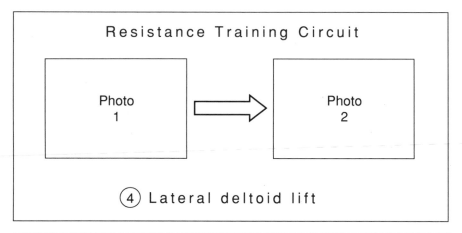

Figure A.6   A sample resistance-training circuit card.

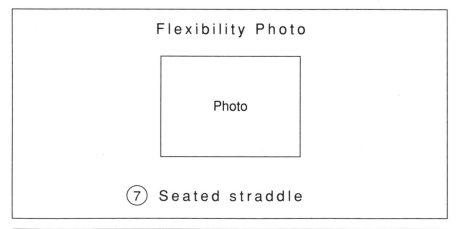

Figure A.7   A sample flexibility photo card.

After the film is developed, follow the directions on pages 144-146 to mount the photographs (as shown in Figure A.7) on cards for use on cones.

Making Task Cards

This section explains how to make cards for these 11 activities:

- Aerobic Task Card
- Pennant Fever
- Run-and-Touch Task Card
- Color-Coded Exercises
- Exercise Task Card
- Group Secret Exercises
- Individual Secret Exercises
- Flexibility Tag
- Flexibility Task Card
- Magic Box
- Secret Stretches

Materials

Assorted index cards (3 by 5, 4 by 6, and 5 by 8 inches), colored markers, and laminating machine.

Procedure

Write, draw, or paste the directions, pictures, or exercise names on the index card. Decorate the card as desired. Write the name of any activity the card is used for somewhere on the card to help you keep cards organized. Laminate the cards. (Samples of many cards are in chapters 4, 5, and 6.)

Making Other Items

This section explains how to make the materials necessary for these seven activities:

- Map Reading and Run
- Pennant Fever

- Fitness Bag
- Fitnopoly
- Magic Box
- Muscle Match
- Stretch-N-Go

Map Reading and Run

Materials

Blank white paper, colored markers, photocopier, and laminating machine.

Procedure

1. Draw a map of the grounds at your facility. Include landmarks the children recognize.
2. Make multiple copies of the map.
3. Using a colored marker draw a running path on each map. Make each path slightly different so that children are not all running to the same place at the same time.
4. Laminate the paper. (You may want to mount the map on card stock before laminating it to make it stiffer.)

Pennant Fever

Materials

10 wooden stakes, 3 to 4 feet long (available at a lumber yard for under $1 each); heavy-duty stapler; construction paper of assorted colors; colored markers; and laminating machine.

Procedure

1. Cut 10 large triangles from the construction paper as shown in Figure A.8. (You may want to mount the triangle on a piece of card stock to make it stiffer.)
2. Number the triangles 1 through 10 and laminate each one.
3. Staple a triangle to the top of each stake.

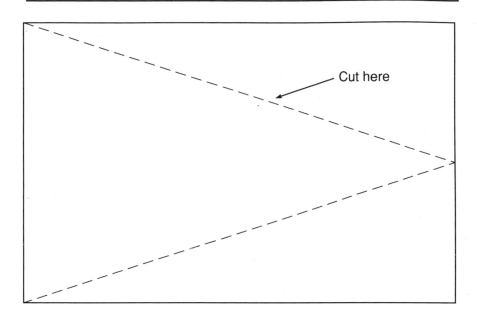

Cut here

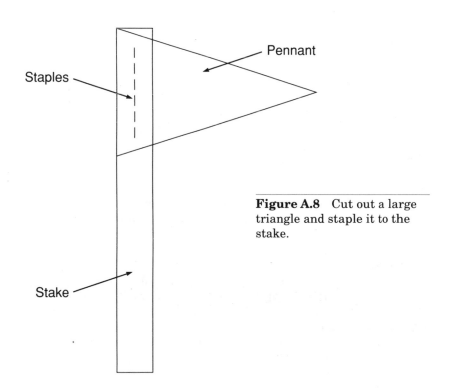

Pennant

Staples

Stake

Figure A.8 Cut out a large triangle and staple it to the stake.

Fitness Bag

Materials

8 to 10 manila envelopes (8-1/2 by 11 inches), 80 to 100 index cards (3 by 5 or 4 by 6 inches), colored markers, laminating machine, and razor-blade knife.

Procedure

1. Decorate the envelope as desired and laminate it. Using the razor blade, slit the lamination at the opening of the envelope so you can open it again.

2. Write an exercise from chapter 3 on the right half of the index card and a number on the left half. Decorate the card as desired and laminate it. Cut the card in half, using different cutting designs and angles, to create a two-piece puzzle (see Figure 5.4, p. 115).

3. Repeat this procedure until you have 10 different exercises in each envelope.

Fitnopoly

Materials

24- by 18-inch poster board, construction paper of assorted colors, colored markers, scissors, glue, and laminating machine.

Procedure

1. Cut out assorted colored circles 2 to 3 inches in diameter (squares and triangles are OK, too). Number the circles from 1 to 30. Label #1 *Start* and #30 *Finish*. Write an exercise or activity you want the children to do on each of the other circles.

2. Glue the circles onto the poster board in numerical order.

3. Using the colored markers, write "Fitnopoly" in the open space near the center of the board. Decorate the rest of the board as you'd like (see Figure 5.5, p. 117).

4. Laminate the board.

Magic Box

Materials

Cardboard box (about 12 by 12 by 12 inches), tape, razor-blade knife, and colored construction paper and glue or paint and paintbrush.

Procedure

1. Tape the box closed and cut an opening in the top large enough to easily put your hand in and pull out a card.
2. Decorate the box with paint or construction paper as desired.
3. Place the magic box task cards (see Figure 6.4, p. 136) inside the box.

Muscle Match

Materials

5- by 8-inch index cards, colored markers, blank white paper, glue, a photocopier, a laminating machine, and a book illustrating stretches. (Several books on the market show drawings or photographs of various stretches. Check the fitness section of any bookstore to find one. You can also draw from photographs you take.)

Procedure

1. Using a picture of a child standing in the anatomical position, trace the outline of the child on a piece of paper. To make it a front view, draw a face and point the feet toward the viewer. To make it a back view, color in the head with hair and point the feet away from the viewer.
2. Make multiple copies of the tracing. You may need to enlarge or reduce the size of the drawing for it to fit on the index card.
3. Cut out each traced copy and glue it to the left half of an index card.
4. Find illustrations of the stretches you want the children to do and trace their outlines on blank paper. Again, you may need to enlarge or reduce the illustrations to fit them on index cards.

5. Cut out each traced copy and glue it to the right half of an index card.

6. Using a marker, in the left body diagram color the muscle that is being stretched in the picture on the right (see Figure 6.5, p. 138).

7. Write the name of the stretching exercise on the back of each card, leaving space so that no letter is positioned in the center of the card (so it doesn't get cut in Step 9).

8. Laminate the card.

9. Cut the card in half, between the two pictures.

Stretch-N-Go

Materials

24- by 18-inch poster board, colored markers, blank white paper, glue, a photocopier, a laminating machine, and a book illustrating stretches. (Several books on the market show drawings or photographs of various stretches. Check the fitness section of any bookstore to find one.)

Procedure

1. Find illustrations of the stretches you want the children to do and trace their outlines on blank paper. You may have to enlarge or reduce the illustrations on a photocopier to fit them on your poster.

2. Cut out each traced copy and glue it onto the poster. Follow this procedure for every stretching exercise you want to include.

3. Using colored markers, write the name of each stretch next to the illustration. Decorate the poster as desired (see Figure 6.6, p. 142).

4. Laminate the poster.

Determining Beats Per Minute

For several activities in chapter 4 you need music with a tempo that matches the type of exercise to be performed. You can determine tempo by counting how many beats occur in one minute.

Listen to the predominant accent in the song you wish to use. For 1 minute, count how many of these "predominant" beats you hear. That is the "bpm." (You can also get a fairly accurate count if you do it for 30 seconds and double the number.)

Glossary

abduction—Movement away from the midline of the body.

adduction—Movement toward the midline of the body.

aerobic exercise—Exercise that requires a large supply of oxygen and improves the efficiency of the heart and lungs to transport oxygen.

aerobic dance—Sequential patterns of movement and exercises performed to music.

agility—The ability to stop and change directions quickly.

anaerobic exercise—Exercise that requires no oxygen.

ballistic stretching—Stretching muscles by using active movement while in a static stretch position. Usually referred to as "bouncing." Not recommended as a way to improve flexibility.

body composition—The ratio of lean body mass to body fat.

cardiac output—The amount of blood pumped by the heart every minute.

cardiorespiratory endurance—The ability of the heart and lungs to supply oxygen to the working muscles for an extended period.

circuit training—A method of training that uses a series of stations, set up in sequential order, to condition different body parts.

concentric contraction—The shortening phase of the muscle fibers in a muscular contraction.

conditioning phase—The core of a workout in which fitness levels are maintained or improved.

continuous training—A method of training, in which the same activity is continued over an extended period.

cool-down—The last phase of a workout, in which the body is allowed to gradually slow down.

dumbbells—Hand-held weights used for resistance training.

duration—The length of time spent participating in an exercise episode.

dynamic stretching—Moving a joint through a full range of motion to stretch its muscles.

eccentric contraction—The lengthening phase of the muscle fibers during a muscular contraction.

extension—Increasing the angle of a joint.

flexibility—The range of motion of a joint.

flexion—Decreasing the angle of a joint.

frequency—How often one engages in exercise activity.

health-related fitness—Fitness related to a person's risk for developing degenerative conditions (e.g., cardiovascular disease, obesity, low back disorders).

heart monitor—A device used to record heart rate during exercise.

high-impact aerobics—A form of aerobic dance in which the feet lose contact with the floor between movements.

intensity—How hard an exercise or exercise episode is performed.

interval training—A method of training that uses short bursts of high-intensity exercise with bouts of rest in between.

intervals—A short burst of high-intensity exercise during interval training.

isometric exercise—An exercise using muscular contractions in which the muscle fibers contract but the joint does not move.

isotonic exercise—An exercise using muscular contractions in which the muscle fibers shorten and lengthen.

Karvonen method—A formula used to calculate target heart rate zone, based on 220 – age as the maximum heart rate.

lifestyle—The decisions a person makes regarding how she or he wishes to live.

low-impact aerobics—A form of aerobic dance in which one foot is always in contact with the floor during movements.

maximum heart rate—The highest possible number of beats the heart can achieve in one minute.

muscular endurance—The ability of a muscle to sustain a contraction, or make multiple contractions, over an extended period.

muscular strength—The amount of force a muscle can exert in a single contraction.

obesity—Having excess body fat.

overload—Exposing the body to greater amounts of exercise than it's accustomed to.

pace—The rate of speed a person travels in relation to the distance being covered.

physical fitness—The condition of the human body and its ability to perform activity.

power—The combination of strength and speed.

progression—The process of gradually increasing the work (frequency, intensity, and/ or duration) in an exercise or activity that helps lead to improvement.

proprioceptive neuromuscular facilitation—Also known as *PNF stretching*. A method of using isometric contractions to help facilitate the range of motion of a joint. It involves working with a partner.

range of motion—The degree of flexibility of a joint.

repetitions—The number of times an exercise is completed in a set.

resistance—The amount of force applied against a muscle or muscles.

set—A series of repetitions.

skinfold calipers—A device used to measure subcutaneous fatty tissue.

specificity—A training principle that focuses exercise on one particular component of fitness, one goal, or one type of training.

sprint—An all-out, full-speed effort.

static stretching—A method of stretching in which the muscle is stretched and held in a tense position for 10 to 60 seconds.

station—A particular exercise in a circuit.

step aerobics—A form of aerobic exercise that uses a platform as a resistance to help elevate the heart rate.

stroke volume—The amount of blood the heart can pump in one beat.

target heart rate zone—The range of heart rate needed to achieve a training effect.

time—The duration one spends in an exercise episode.

training effect—The amount of exercise needed to show improvement in a fitness component.

warm-up—The beginning phase of an exercise episode, used to raise the heart rate and generate blood flow to the muscles.

weight training—A form of exercise that uses resistance to improve muscular strength and endurance.

References

American College of Sports Medicine. (1990). The recommended quantity and quality of exercise for developing and maintaining cardiorespiratory and muscular fitness in healthy adults. *Medicine and Science in Sports and Exercise*, **22**(2), 265-274.

Cahill, B. (Ed.) (1988). *Proceedings of the conference on strength training and the prepubescent*. Chicago: American Orthopaedic Society for Sports Medicine.

Hinson, C. (1994). Pulse power: A heart physiology program for children. *Journal of Physical Education, Recreation & Dance*, **65**(1), 62-68.

Karvonen, J.J., Kentala, E., & Mustala, O. (1957). The effects of training on the heart rate. *Annales Medicinae Experimentalis et Biologiae Fenniae*, **35**, 307-315.

Maslow, A.H. (1971). *The farther reaches of human nature*. New York: Penguin.

Mosston, M., & Ashworth, S. (1990). *The spectrum of teaching styles: From command to discovery*. New York: Longman.

Pate, R. (1983). A new definition of youth fitness. *Physician and Sports Medicine*, **11**(4), 80.

Raffini, J.P. (1993). *Winners without losers: Structures and strategies for increasing student motivation to learn*. Boston: Allyn and Bacon.

Rowland, T.W. (1990). *Exercise and children's health*. Champaign, IL: Human Kinetics.

About the Author

Curt Hinson is a physical education specialist at Lancashire Elementary School in Wilmington, Delaware. He received his MEd from Widener University in 1989.

Hinson uses his more than 10 years of experience in the classroom to write "Tips From the Trenches," a regular column featured in *Teaching Elementary Physical Education (TEPE)* since 1991. In addition, he has published articles on elementary school fitness and made numerous presentations at conferences around the country.

Hinson was the 1991-92 Delaware Elementary Physical Education Teacher of the Year, the 1992 Eastern District COPEC Physical Education Teacher of the Year, and a finalist for the 1992 National Elementary Physical Education Teacher of the Year.

Hinson, who is past vice-president of the Delaware Association for Health, Physical Education, Recreation and Dance, also is a member of the American Alliance for Health, Physical Education, Recreation and Dance, Council on Physical Education for Children, National Association for Sport and Physical Education, and National Dance Association.